Contents

ACKNOWLEDGEMENTS   i
LIST OF FIGURES   ii
LIST OF TABLES   iii

CHAPTER I INTRODUCTION   1
    Electricity Futures: America's Economic Imperative   1
    Purpose and Scope of the Study   1
    Recent Trends in Electricity Use   2
    Lessons of the Past-Forecasts in the Early 1960s   4
    Patterns for the Future   7

CHAPTER II THE FUTURE CONTEXT FOR
ENERGY AND ELECTRICITY USE   9
    Major Forces Affecting the U.S. Socioeconomic Landscape Over the
    Next 25 Years   9
    Changing Demographic Characteristics of the Population   10
    Shifting Currents in the Economy   19
    Continuing Integration of the International Economic System 27
    Escalating Competition and Intensifying Product Cycles   34
    Patterns of Life: Industry, Commerce and Households   41
    The Sociopolitical Atmosphere   49

CHAPTER III. FUTURE ENERGY AND ELECTRICITY DEMAND:
THE 1990S THROUGH 2015   57
    The Project's Reference Case Forecast   57
    Major Forces Influencing Residential Energy Demand   66
    Widespread Efficiency Moves Residential Forecasts   68
    Major Forces Influencing Commercial Energy Demand   73
    Commercial Forecast Reflects Refined Uses   77
    Major Forces Influencing Industrial Energy Demand   83
    New Applications Balance Efficiency in Industrial Forecast 88
    Major Forces Influencing Transportation Energy Demand   97
    Market Opportunities for Electricity   100
    Transportation Forecast Shows Steady Electricity Gain   102
    Alternative Developments that Could Make a Difference   103

APPENDIX A OVERVIEW OF THE PROJECT'S FORECASTING
    APPROACH   107

APPENDIX B FURTHER FORECAST RESULTS   115

Acknowledgements

The Electricity Futures Project is conducted under the sponsorship of the Edison Electric Institute and directed by the EEI Strategic Planning Department and the EEI Economics Committee. EEI gratefully acknowledges the contributions of the Electric Power Research Institute, the North American Electric Reliability Council, the Battelle Memorial Institute, the Interindustry Economic Research Fund at the University of Maryland, the Strategic Decisions Group, and The Futures Group. Mark Broush and Peter Stern of The Futures Group were principally responsible for integrating a great deal of material provided by the other participants along with their own research to create the complete draft report. The members of the EEI Economics Committee conceptualized the project, made substantial direct contributions, and provided rigorous review of successive drafts.

List of Figures

Figure 1.1   Growth Rates in Electricity Use and GNP
      1.2   U.S. Electricity Use
      1.3   Electricity Use Ratios

      2.1   Future U.S. Population Growth
      2.2   Ethnic Mix of U.S. Population
      2.3A-B Forecasted U.S. Population   14-
      2.4   Projected U.S. Regional Populations 1990-2010
      2.5   U.S. Households
      2.6   Average U.S. Household Size
      2.7   Trends in Growth of Output
      2.8   Trends in Growth of Income
      2.9   Trend in Growth of U.S. Productivity
      2.10-11 International Comparisons   24-
      2.12   Balances in Trade and the Federal Budget
      2.13   Components of the Saving-Investment Balance
      2.14   Trends in Income
      2.15   Growth in Labor Productivity Vs.Growth in Capital
      2.16   Gross Domestic Product Growth Vs.Rate of Savings
      2.17   U.S. Trends in Output Composition
      2.18   U.S. Trends in Employment Composition

      3.1   End Use Energy - U.S. Total
      3.2   Comparative Growth Trends
      3.3   The Future U.S. Economy
      3.4   Energy Use in the Residential Sector
      3.5   Residential Energy Intensity by End Use
      3.6   Energy Use in the Commercial Sector
      3.7   Commercial Energy Intensity by End Use
      3.8   Growth in Commercial Floor Space
      3.9   Energy Intensity by Commercial Segment
      3.10   Energy Use in the Industrial Sector
      3.11   Industrial Energy Intensity by End Use
      3.12A-B Growth in Industrial Output   94-
      3.13A-B Energy Intensity by Industrial Segment   96-
      3.14   Energy Use in Transportation
      3.15   Major Electricity Uses in Transportation   1

List of Tables

Table	2.1	Productivity Growth by Industry Sector	23
	2.2	Areas of New Technology with Major Economic Impact 1988-2000	31
	2.3	Sectoral Composition of New Jobs in the U.S. Economy	39
	2.4	The Potential for U.S. GNP Growth Over the Next 25 Years	42
	2.5	Technology and Processes for the Factory of the Future	45
	2.6	Opportunities for Improving Productivity in Service Industries	46
	2.7	Occupational Trends to the Year 2000	48
	3.1	Residential Sector Energy and Electricity for End Use	58
	3.2	Forecast Totals Sectoral Mix of Electricity Requirements	60
	3.3	Key Characteristics of the Future Economy	63
	3.4	Residential Sector Energy and Electricity for End Use	65
	3.5	Residential Sector Trend in Shares of End Use Categories	69
	3.6	Commercial Sector Energy and Electricity for End Use	74
	3.7	Commercial Sector Segments Distinguished	80
	3.8	Industrial Sector Energy and Electricity for End Use	85
	3.9	Industrial Sector Segments Distinguished in the Study	93
	3.10	Transportation Sector Historical Energy and Electricity Consumption	98
	3.11	Transportation Sector Energy and Electricity for End Use	98
	3.12	Transportation Sector Major Components of Electricity Use	104

CHAPTER I.

Introduction

ELECTRICITY FUTURES: AMERICA'S ECONOMIC IMPERATIVE

Electricity has become essential to the American economy. It powers the nation's productivity and it sustains living standards and lifestyles. It also accounts for an ever-growing share of total energy requirements because it is uniquely adaptable to new technology.

The future of electricity growth is less clear. Will this country's dependence on it continue to grow, and, if so, at what rate? How will coming changes in the way Americans use energy to achieve social and economic goals affect the country's requirements for electric power as the 21st century nears?

PURPOSE AND SCOPE OF THE STUDY

The Edison Electric Institute's Electricity Futures Project has begun to address these questions through exploration of a scenario that represents the playing out of a number of forces that will shape the social, economic and energy future of the United States. The Project's findings are presented in this report.

The economic future envisioned by the Project's scenario is vibrant, with gross domestic product per capita and labor productivity growing faster than in the past. Commercial and industrial growth, increasingly reliant on electricity, will be healthy in a world of vigorous international competition and rapidly changing technology.

The close tracking of electricity and real Gross National

Product (GNP) growth rates, so evident since the mid-1970 will persist through the year 2000. Beyond 2000, however, th relationship can be expected to change under the influence higher electricity prices, improving end-use efficiency and stru tural changes in the composition of the U.S. economy. Despi slowing electricity growth, the share of electricity in the nation energy profile will continue to expand. Improving energy eff ciency and greater electrification will continue hand-in-hand. I short, electricity will become increasingly imperative to th nation's economy.

The scenario described in the following pages is not destin however. The future that does emerge also will be affected b economic, political, demographic and technological events an choices that cannot be anticipated. Nevertheless, the forces work are powerful and have potential implications that deman attention.

RECENT TRENDS IN ELECTRICITY USE

Electricity use patterns over the past 20 years reveal a shar relationship between the nation's productivity and how muc electricity Americans use. Invariably, as the GNP rises and fall so does electricity use, especially since the energy turmoil of th 1970s. Figure 1.1 dramatically illustrates this relationship, phenomenon that analysts have observed for some time an affects predictions of future electricity use. This pattern contin ued to persist even after the 1970s when the growth in electric us clearly outpaced GNP growth. The reasons behind the stron growth that came later are the convergence of a powerful baby boom housing market with a rapidly growing labor force, th spread of air-conditioning in both residential and commercia markets and the declining price of electricity.

Electricity held its own during the energy retrenchment years While OPEC price increases, beginning in 1973, drained th domestic economy and caused recessions especially among in dustry, energy conservation affected the direct-use fuels far mor drastically than it did electricity. The shift in manufacturing awa from the energy-intensive industries to the less-intensive one caused a decline in petroleum and gas usage, while new electri applications grew despite more high-efficiency equipment an operational improvements. Electric use was also buttressed by buoyant commercial sector that kept adding floor space a residential construction receded due to the inflation-drive recession of the early 1980s. The "coupling" of GNP and electri growth rates after 1974 has been maintained to the present rough recession and prosperity. Yet, it is unclear whether this lationship will continue into the future.

Figure 1.2 traces growth in electric use within principal sectors f the economy. Notably, between 1965 and 1976 total use oubled despite a short period of arrested growth in the mid-970s. Then, the years following the post-OPEC experience, 976-87, led to a mere 25 percent increase. While electric onsumption in the residential sector appears to have withstood ie price dislocations, the commercial and industrial sectors did ot, and in 1982 electricity experienced its first year of absolute ecline in demand since the Depression.

Figure 1.3 illustrates the same historical trends with different ata. The per capita use of electricity grew steeply until 1973, esponded to the two price shocks, then moved more irregularly id now reflects an uptilt that may mark the resurgence of manu-icturing. When measured for its contribution to the value of all oods and services produced in the United States, electricity ems to be following a steady course at about 1/2 kilowatt hour cwh) per GNP dollar (costing, on average, 2-3 cents in that

FIGURE 1.1

GROWTH RATES IN ELECTRICITY USE AND GNP

CHANGE OVER PREVIOUS YEAR

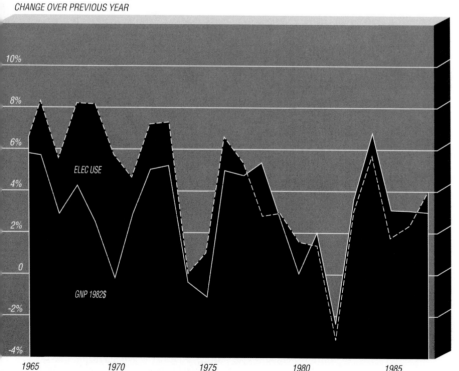

10%

8%

6%

ELEC USE

4%

2%

0

GNP 1982$

-2%

-4%

1965   1970   1975   1980   1985

Source: based on Edison Electric Institute statistics for elelectricity use and economic statistics from The Economic Report of the President, 1988.

period). Whether these relationships can be maintained in the future, as the drive for energy efficiency competes with innovative uses for electricity, underlies much of the forecast discussion in Chapter 3.

LESSONS OF THE PAST—FORECASTS IN THE EARLY 1960s

A brief look at energy forecasts in the Fifties and Sixties offers a unique perspective and an opportunity to re-examine projections made when the future seemed secure and predictable.

The first comprehensive and thoughtful postwar study of the nation's resource needs was released in 1952. Entitled *Resources for Freedom*, the report of the President's Commission on Materials Policy came to be known as the Paley Commission Report. The Commission believed long-term economic growth was both feasible and desirable; technology could overcome

FIGURE 1.2
U.S. ELECTRICITY USE

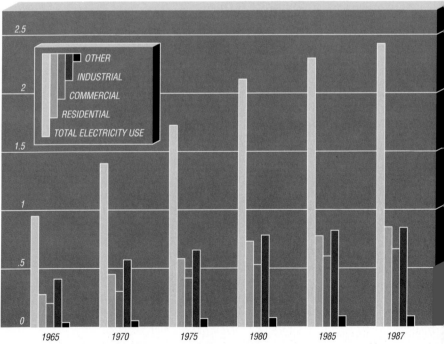

MILLIONS OF KILOWATT HOURS

OTHER
INDUSTRIAL
COMMERCIAL
RESIDENTIAL
TOTAL ELECTRICITY USE

2.5
2
1.5
1
.5
0

1965   1970   1975   1980   1985   1987

Source: Edison Electric Institute

Notes: Purchases by sector are figures reported by EEI as "sales to ultimate customers." Industry is "large power and light" accounts; commercial is "small power and light" accounts; both series are not directly comparable on year-to-year basis due to classification shifts. Figures for self-generated power are for on-site consumption only; available figures do not distinguish industrial and commercial self generation.

ıblic perceptions about the depletion of nonrenewable re-
urces. The "running out" theme sounded by conservationists
ıs overruled by the economic argument that, at a cost, there is
ways more and that technological innovation is the agent for
ıshing depletion into the future. It is the choice of technology
at matters, since cost constraints do not permit striking out in
ı directions at one time.

Even with its confidence in economic growth, the Paley Com-
ıission significantly underestimated many of the parameters of
ostwar expansion. It failed to anticipate the baby boom, project-
g the country's population to rise from 151 million in 1950 to
ıst 193 million in 1975 (actual 1975 population was 216
ıillion). Its forecast of labor force growth also was short—from
ı million in 1950 to 82 million in 1975. The correct figure
rned out to be 95 million, due in large part to the unanticipated
ıe in the number of working women. The work week was
.pected to decline by 15 percent and productivity to grow at a
eady 2.5 percent per year. Instead, the work week declined by

THOUSANDS OF KILOWATT HOURS PER CAPITA, PER GNP 82$

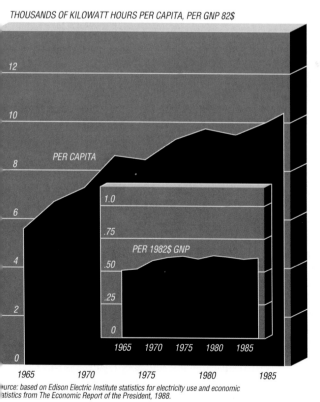

FIGURE 1.3
**ELECTRICITY
USE
RATIOS**

ıurce: based on Edison Electric Institute statistics for electricity use and economic
ıtistics from The Economic Report of the President, 1988.

less than 10 percent and productivity rose, on average, by
percent per year. As a result, GNP over the quarter centur
increased at an average annual rate of 3.3 percent, some 1
percent faster than forecast.

In energy, the Commission foresaw demand doubling be
tween 1950 and 1975 in lockstep with the rise in GNP. It furthe
projected that liquid fuel use would more than double, co
consumption would rise by 40-60 percent and the demand fo
electricity (from all energy sources but with nuclear not yet
factor) and natural gas triple at the very least. Here, too, th
Commission's expectations proved to be conservative, especiall
when electricity demand actually quintupled in kilowatt hou
sales by utilities over that quarter century.

The Paley Report remained a remarkable policy-guidin
document for many years because it carved out a fertile enviror
ment for the economies of scale and the technologies of subst
tution to meet the materials needs of a fast-growing, increasing
affluent society. The technological optimism of the document–
written in the "Atoms for Peace" era—starkly contrasts with th
cautionary and questioning mood of a post-Vietnam generatio
beset by concerns over the environmental and health effects o
developing technologies.

By the 1960s, the Federal Power Commission (FPC) ha
assumed the responsibility for reporting on the electric powe
industry's outlook. Its 1964 survey projected a near doubling i
per capita electricity consumption between 1963 and 1980
based on the rapid spread of electric cooling and heating system
in homes, business and industry. The 1970 survey revised tha
projection upward by 14 percent (to 3 trillion kwh), arguing tha
demand would build up much faster than anticipated in 196
because of declining costs and more electric appliances. Th
1970 FPC survey also foresaw 1990 electricity use almost doubl
from 1980, representing an annual growth rate of 7 percent.

In retrospect, 1980 sales amounted to less than 2.2 trillio
kwh. Even 1987 sales, at 2.5 trillion kwh, lagged behind th
forecasted 1980 level by 16 percent. And the FPC 1990 target o
almost 6 trillion kwh, more than twice now expected for that yea
stands as the last of the dynamic extrapolations fashioned out o
the 1960s.

By the early 1970s, analysts had begun to question th
feasibility of a decennial doubling of the U.S. power supply. Ye
the FPC found it:

> ...paradoxical that at a time when many individuals are
> calling for curtailment of power growth in the interests of
> environmental protection, the best judgment of those

whose business is to study demand trends is that the nation's electrical requirements will very nearly quadruple between 1970 and 1990. (The 1970 National Power Survey, pp. I.1-13).

The price shocks of the 1970s would temper these forecasts which, made in a time of declining costs, did not (and could not) anticipate consumer response to the rising cost of electricity. In 1968, the average unit price stood at 1.54 cents per kwh. The 1964 survey had projected it to decline to 1.2 cents by 1980. The 1970 survey, anticipating fuel price increases and the end of further economies of scale, estimated 1990 prices to ultimate consumers at 1.83 cents/kwh (in 1968 dollars), close to the average retail price in the late 1980s, when adjusted for 20 years of inflation. Given the events of the 1970s and early 1980s, it is indeed remarkable that electric rates have not significantly outrun inflation.

In estimating future electric generation requirements, the FPC 1970 survey used a 20 percent reserve margin to set 1980 capacity requirements at 665 gigawatts and 1990 requirements at almost twice that level. By the end of 1970, the nation had installed generating capacity of almost 340 gigawatts. The survey thus called for a doubling of capacity during the 1970s and another doubling in the 1980s. Clearly, had the industry not applied the brakes on new construction in recognition of post-1970 events and the resulting financial constraints, the country would have found itself with far more generating capacity in reserve than it has currently.

While hindsight offers clues to the future, it also illustrates the precarious nature of forecasting. Regardless of persuasive data and trends, unforeseen external events always can derail the best laid forecast. Such events as OPEC actions, the ensuing oil embargo and other external factors have influenced the electric industry's course far more than the industry's own efforts to guide its destiny.

PATTERNS FOR THE FUTURE

The postwar history of electricity has been one of considerable growth tempered but not radically altered by external events and the changing role of the United States in the world economy. Yet, in looking ahead, the recent past cannot be forgotten. While lifestyles, institutions and consumer habits will change more rapidly, their established patterns will shift only gradually.

For all energy requirements, future demand will be dictated by consumer preferences in the home and by a drive for efficiency in the workplace. In the past, the country's productive machine — mass production in the heavy industries—was energy intensive. In the future, with a shift to lower energy intensity in the growing segments of the economy, the emphasis will be on the versatility and efficiency with which energy resources are used. The country's increasing reliance on high technology, specialized manufacturing and information services underlies the expectation that the demand for electricity will continue to grow faster than the demand for primary fuels (except in transportation).

For the United States to remain competitive, energy will have to be both reliable and affordable. Within the next 25 years, the gradual depletion (hence relative cost increase) of oil and natural gas will have to be counteracted by technological and institutional improvements in the delivery of energy in a form manageable to consumers.

The demand for electricity cannot be projected independently of price considerations. These, in turn, depend on global imponderables. Since this study reaches well into the 21st century, the relative cost of electricity will be affected not only by what happens to the price of oil and other energy sources, but also by the costs associated with existing, replacement and new capacity facilities, including the cost of demand-side management investments. Its course also will be shaped by the investment decisions of the suppliers of electricity, whatever their corporate structure or regulatory status. Thus the interplay between resource decisions and market demand, based on clear price signals, represents the central challenge to the industry's strategic planning efforts

CHAPTER II.

The Future Context for Energy and Electricity Use

MAJOR FORCES AFFECTING THE U.S. SOCIOECONOMIC LANDSCAPE OVER THE NEXT 25 YEARS

To make reasonable assumptions about the growth of consumer energy requirements, forecasters must step back and assess the forces and circumstances that will affect decisionmakers' behavior in the future. As in the past, the demand for electricity will be strongly influenced by the dynamics of the economy; the relationship between aggregate measures of economic growth and energy demand will continue to be important. Other influences are at work as well, and the full impact of some is difficult to quantify. As experience has proved with the OPEC embargoes and the emergence of environmental awareness, departures from trends can be far more significant for the energy outlook than changes in the terms of trade or the relative energy intensity of individual industry groups.

This chapter explores those characteristics of the nation's socioeconomic landscape most likely to influence energy choices within the study's time horizon. The broad trends that are forecasted are not always tied to anticipated levels of demand. Yet this environmental scanning should provide common ground and a qualitative context to make quantitative assumptions and fashion inputs for long-term forecasting models.

The next 25 years may change more rapidly than the past quarter-century. Potent demographic and economic forces will define the nation's growth. Technological advances portend an information-based era that will enhance the bases for business and private decisions and enrich lifestyle choices. Other develop-

ments, especially in global politics, are more speculative but r
less important. These forces are reviewed in the sections th
follow.

CHANGING DEMOGRAPHIC CHARACTERISTICS OF THE POPULATION

Planners and decisionmakers often assume that the futu
pattern of population growth is the one socioeconomic variab
that can be predicted with reasonable certainty. Convention
wisdom has it that the U.S. demographic record is so comple
that accurate projections are quite feasible with only a narro
band of uncertainty. Only migration, the third component
demographic change, is the wild card in fashioning projections
being conditioned by public policy and by differences in ec
nomic opportunity between nations.

Solid as population statistics may be, it still is not possible

FIGURE 2.1
FUTURE U.S. POPULATION GROWTH

MILLIONS OF PERSONS

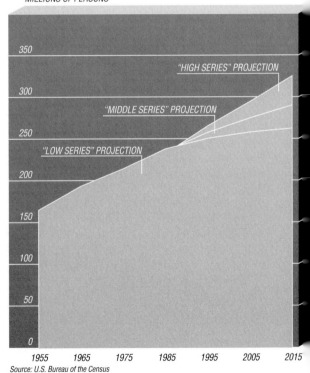

"HIGH SERIES" PROJECTION

"MIDDLE SERIES" PROJECTION

"LOW SERIES" PROJECTION

350

300

250

200

150

100

50

0

1955   1965   1975   1985   1995   2005   2015

Source: U.S. Bureau of the Census

stablish a reliable figure for the nation's total population in the
ear 2000. With just 11 years to go, the fan of uncertainty for
000 brackets 25-30 million people, the equivalent of the entire
opulation of California (see Figure 2.1). When the forecast is
xtended to 2015, the bracket spans almost 65 million, more
han today's population of the entire Midwest, reaching from
)hio to Colorado and from the Canadian border to the South.

Nevertheless, reasonable assumptions can be made about the
uture composition of this country. The face of America will be
trifle more wrinkled, surely more multi-hued and cosmopoli-
an, and tilt more to the West and the South. By the year 2015,
he demographic makeup of the United States will be sufficiently
lifferent from what it is today to have a profound influence on
national development and hence on the demand for energy.
ince demand for energy and electricity is derived from diverse
nd uses, it will be affected profoundly by the growth in the

SHARE OF TOTAL POPULATION

FIGURE 2.2
ETHNIC MIX
OF U.S.
POPULATION

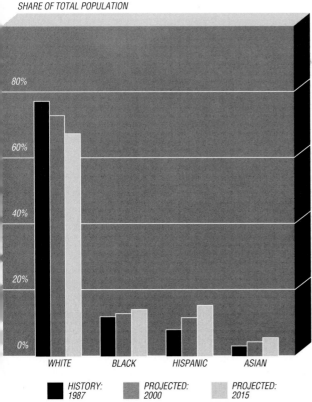

| | HISTORY: 1987 | PROJECTED: 2000 | PROJECTED: 2015 |

Source: U.S. Bureau of the Census, American Council on Life Insurance, The Futures Group.

number of households, their size and makeup, their income and education, their participation in the work force and their geographic distribution. The following sections examine the variables that will affect American households and, ultimately, electricity demand.

FERTILITY

Fertility rates have been declining in all industrialized countries for a long time. This is true in the United States as well, although the post-World War II baby boom brought about a temporary yet significant interruption in the decline, and the "echo boomlet" of that generation is causing yet another gentle resurgence in the annual number of births. Most important for the future, however, is that the total fertility rate of women (i.e., the number of children that women are expected to bear through their reproductive years) now appears insufficient to replace the population. Since 1972, that rate has been below the replacement rate of 2.1 children for each "completed" family. With more and more women entering the labor force and postponing childbearing, there is little likelihood of this reproductive pattern reversing, except for the higher fertility of the principal immigrant groups and the poorer segments of the population, and the lag in limiting family size among the less educated.

On balance, U.S. fertility probably will not rise much beyond the replacement level over the forecast period. The three-child family will no longer be the norm. Even so, fertility rates will ebb and flow somewhat in response to changing income expectations, the number and ethnic composition of future immigrants and the anticipated reduction in adolescent pregnancies.

MORTALITY

Mortality rates have been declining significantly in the past 25 years, as greater emphasis is placed on health-preserving lifestyles and medical research. Life expectancy at birth for males is now moving beyond 70 years and for women it will soon pass the 80-year mark. Mortality rates in the future will not slow as dramatically, as the most intractable causes of death will require vast new resources and longer lead times for further progress. Yet, even with unanticipated reverses in AIDS and drug-related morbidity, the downward trend in mortality will continue.

Because of recent health improvements, particularly in the oldest age groups, the U.S. population is getting older. As low fertility continues to prevail, the population 65 years and older will account for an ever-larger share of the total, probably more than 15 percent by the year 2015. Estimating when mortality rates will level out is the chief uncertainty for this component of population changes.

IMMIGRATION

New entrants to the nation constitute a highly volatile component of growth. They also have a compounding effect because of their predominant youth and higher fertility, particularly among Hispanics. Not since the Depression has immigration (not counting illegal entrants) reached current levels.

For the future, the forecasters assume the United States will accept from 450,000 to 500,000 immigrants a year to about 900,000, which more accurately reflects the current realities of illegal entry and the potential liberalization of immigration policy and residence amnesty. The difference between these two levels of immigration can create a potential spread of more than 11 million in the year 2000 population. Beyond that date, immigration will account for an ever-larger segment of any forecast's uncertainty range.

AGE DISTRIBUTION

The population's future age distribution also is influenced by assumptions about fertility, mortality and migration. But since a significant share of the year 2015 population is alive today (i.e., over 26 years old) and since fertility is unlikely to rise significantly after the turn of the century, the middle-aged working population will make up a much larger share, the young and school-age groups a smaller share, and those 65 years and older a larger share of the total population. (Current expectations for the future age composition of the nation's population, taking into account forecast uncertainties, are traced in Figures 2.3A and 2.3B.)

MINORITIES

With fertility rates higher, on average, among minorities and immigrants than the white population, the stage is set for minorities to make up a larger share of the total population (see Figure 2.2). Blacks, Hispanics and Asians account for under 23 percent of the population at this time; this could become 28 percent by the year 2000. Because of continuing immigration and a marked difference in fertility, the number of people of Hispanic origin could outnumber the Black population as early as the year 2005.

Since at least two-thirds of the immigrants of working age

probably will enter the labor force, the impact of minorities on the regions where they live will be significant. Whether these groups are successfully absorbed into the regional work force or whether the new entrants are attracted to areas with labor shortages, they will influence the geographical distribution of the U.S. population.

GEOGRAPHIC DISTRIBUTION

Almost without respite, the growing U.S. population has been moving away from the older urban areas of the Northeast and the rural Midwest and toward southern and western regions. Patterns of internal migration (i.e., within the United States) change in response to differences in economic opportunity between regions. The longer-term outlook, nevertheless, favors the less-densely settled warmer states and the Far West, which is poised to benefit from the emerging buoyancy of the rapidly growing Pacific Rim economy.

FIGURE 2.3A
FORECASTED U.S. POPULATION

BY YOUNGEST AGE SUBGROUPS

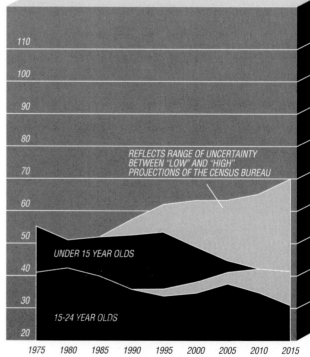

MILLIONS OF PERSONS

REFLECTS RANGE OF UNCERTAINTY BETWEEN "LOW" AND "HIGH" PROJECTIONS OF THE CENSUS BUREAU

UNDER 15 YEAR OLDS

15-24 YEAR OLDS

1975 1980 1985 1990 1995 2000 2005 2010 2015

Source: U.S. Department of Commerce, Bureau of the Census

Surveying the four major regional groupings of states, the Census Bureau anticipates, between now and the year 2010, a continued rapid growth in the West, somewhat more moderate growth in the South, virtually no growth in the Midwest, and a very slow increase in the Northeast. Furthermore, half of the nation's population increase during this period will occur in just California, Texas and Florida. Figure 2.4 summarizes these regional trends.

Internal migration and immigration respond largely to economic opportunity. That is why population redistribution is especially hard to predict, because the factors that cause a region to draw people and resources and another region to give these up are difficult to predict.

A well-established trend, however, is the movement of people and employment centers to the fringes of large metropolitan areas and the rural belts that link these urban centers. Some central cities may succeed in reversing decades of neglect, others will not, but everywhere the success of the future will require

MILLIONS OF PERSONS

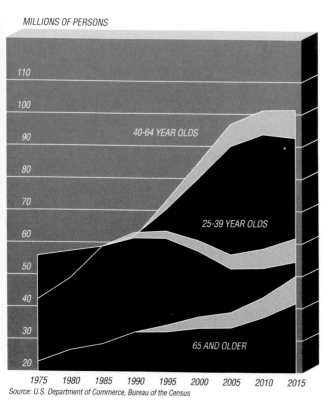

FIGURE 2.3B
FORECASTED U.S. POPULATION

Source: U.S. Department of Commerce, Bureau of the Census

FIGURE 2.4
PROJECTED U.S. REGIONAL POPULATIONS 1990-2010

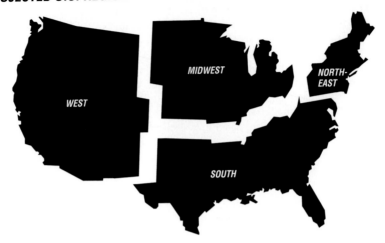

HISTORY/1986
MILLIONS OF PERSONS BY REGION
NORTHEAST
  50.0 MILLION PERSONS
MIDWEST
  59.3 MILLION PERSONS
SOUTH
  83.0 MILLION PERSONS
WEST
  48.8 MILLION PERSONS

PROJECTED/1990
MILLIONS OF PERSONS BY REGION;
AVERAGE ANNUAL REGIONAL GROWTH (1990-2000)
PERCENT CHANGE IN REGION (1990-2000)
NORTHEAST
  50.6 MILLION PERSONS
  0.3% ANNUAL GROWTH
  3.1% GREATER THAN 1980
MIDWEST
  59.8 MILLION PERSONS
  0.2% ANNUAL GROWTH
  1.5% GREATER THAN 1980
SOUTH
  87.3 MILLION PERSONS
  1.5% ANNUAL GROWTH
  15.8% GREATER THAN 1980
WEST
  52.3 MILLION PERSONS
  1.9% ANNUAL GROWTH
  21.1% GREATER THAN 1980

PROJECTED/2000
MILLIONS OF PERSONS BY REGION;
AVERAGE ANNUAL REGIONAL GROWTH (1990-2000)
PERCENT CHANGE IN REGION (1990-2000)
NORTHEAST
  51.8 MILLION PERSONS
  0.2% ANNUAL GROWTH
  2.4% GREATER THAN 1990
MIDWEST
  59.6 MILLION PERSONS
  0% ANNUAL GROWTH
  -0.3% LESS THAN 1990
SOUTH
  96.9 MILLION PERSONS
  1.0% ANNUAL GROWTH
  11% GREATER THAN 1990
WEST
  59.4 MILLION PERSONS
  1.3% ANNUAL GROWTH
  13.6% GREATER THAN 1990

PROJECTED/2010
MILLIONS OF PERSONS BY REGION;
AVERAGE ANNUAL REGIONAL GROWTH (2000-2010)
PERCENT CHANGE IN REGION (2000-2010)
NORTHEAST
  52.5 MILLION PERSONS
  0.1% ANNUAL GROWTH
  1.4% GREATER THAN 2000
MIDWEST
  59.0 MILLION PERSONS
  -0.1% ANNUAL GROWTH
  -1.0% LESS THAN 2000
SOUTH
  104.9 MILLION PERSONS
  0.8% ANNUAL GROWTH
  8.3% GREATER THAN 2000
WEST
  65.6 MILLION PERSONS
  1.0% ANNUAL GROWTH
  10.4% GREATER THAN 2000

Source: U.S. Dept. of Commerce, Bureau of the Census.

better linkages between the areas of job creation and the places where people live. Important, too, will be the matching of working skills with employment opportunities within a labor market area.

HOUSEHOLDS

Households will continue to be the basic social unit whose needs and lifestyles drive the economy. Reflecting the dramatic changes in family structures and living patterns, the number of people per household will decline from about 2.7 today to perhaps 2.35 in 2015. This trend is due to a lower birth rate and to the continuing increase in the number of households occupied by single adults. Figures 2.5 and 2.6 depict the anticipated future trends for both the number and types of households and the average household size.

The instability of the contemporary family, the proclivity of young adults and the elderly to live independently and the high incidence of households with only one parent all account for a living pattern that may not have been predicted prior to the social changes of the 1960s. Obviously, there will be a limit to "downsizing." The number of adults per household will probably not decline after 2000, but the average number of children will continue to fall as more women enter the labor force and postpone births.

WORK FORCE

Demographic trends shape the work force. The post-World War II baby boom caused an unprecedented increase in the number of people in the labor force beginning in the late 1960s. That wave has run its course and the nation's declining fertility points to a shortage rather than a surplus of new workers in the decades ahead. In fact, the labor force is expected to increase more slowly than at any time since the 1930s. Its annual growth rate should be a mere 1 percent in the 1990s, as compared with more than 2 percent in the 1970s and early 1980s.

The characteristics of that work force will change as well, with important implications for the nation's economy. These are the changes that will be most noteworthy between now and the year 2000:

•The work force will be getting older, and the availability of younger workers will decline. In fact, by 2000 the 15-24 age group will likely be smaller by some 2 million than at present.

•More women will be entering the labor force even though female working rates already have been rising steadily since the

1950s. Almost 70 percent of all entrants will be women who, by 2000, will account for almost half the total work force (compared with one-third in 1960). Their participation rate will be so high (61 percent versus 38 percent in 1960) that fertility rates could drop even more if child-rearing requirements cannot be met by employers or supported by society.

• Minorities and immigrants will constitute a growing share of the entrants into the labor force. The decline in the total number of young workers offers a window of opportunity for these groups to be fully absorbed into the economy. The challenge is to equip these new entrants with the knowledge and skills required by a rapidly changing job market. More than 40 percent of the entrants between now and the year 2000 will be minority immigrants, and that share could be larger if immigration levels continue to rise.

FIGURE 2.5
U.S.
HOUSEHOLDS

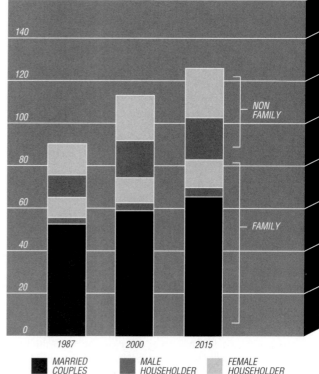

HOUSEHOLDS (MILLIONS), BY TYPE

MARRIED COUPLES MALE HOUSEHOLDER FEMALE HOUSEHOLDER

Source: U.S. Department of Commerce, Bureau of the Census; The Futures Group.

SHIFTING CURRENTS IN THE ECONOMY

The recent performance and growth of the U.S. economy mixes positive developments with some worrisome trends. The nation's economic future will be determined in large measure by how well the positives can be accentuated and the negative elements corrected.

On the positive side, the nation continues to ride the upward sweep of a sustained and powerful cyclical expansion—the financial crash of October 1987 notwithstanding. Of particular importance, this expansion has been marked by a significant strengthening of real growth in economic output, income and labor productivity. Figures 2.7, 2.8, 2.9 and Table 2.1 illustrate these trends for several key measures of economic performance. Rates of change in all of these areas had been sharply down since the late 1970s and generally sluggish since the mid-1960s.

Since 1981, the nation has enjoyed an average growth rate of real GNP that is on a par with or exceeds that of the other major

NUMBER OF PERSONS PER HOUSEHOLD

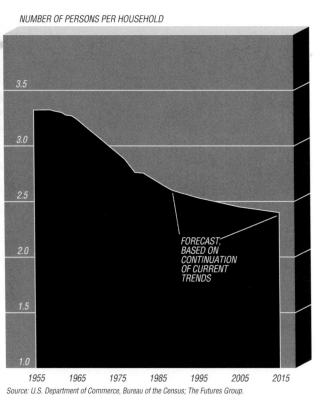

FIGURE 2.6
AVERAGE U.S. HOUSEHOLD SIZE

FORECAST, BASED ON CONTINUATION OF CURRENT TRENDS

Source: U.S. Department of Commerce, Bureau of the Census; The Futures Group.

industrialized nations (Figure 2.10). Comparatively, the U.S. standard of living—as measured by output per capita—remains well above that of the other leading industrialized nations, including Japan and West Germany (Figure 2.11).

With respect to employment, the nation has led the world in job creation. Between 1955 and 1986, the United States created 47.4 million new jobs—Japan, by contrast, created 16.6 million and the European Community only 5.7 million. Indeed, during the current expansion, evidence indicates that rising U.S. employment has been particularly broad across the spectrum of society, including groups traditionally out of the labor market, such as minorities and youths. And the U.S. unemployment rate is now in the mid-5 percent range, while that of many European nations is twice as high or even higher.

These upbeat trends are significant. They are balanced, however, by evidence of emerging weaknesses in the nation's economic capabilities which, at the very least, raise questions about prospects for the future.

FIGURE 2.7
**TRENDS
IN GROWTH
OF OUTPUT**

ANNUAL CHANGE. 4 YEAR MOVING AVERAGE
CONSTANT 1982 $

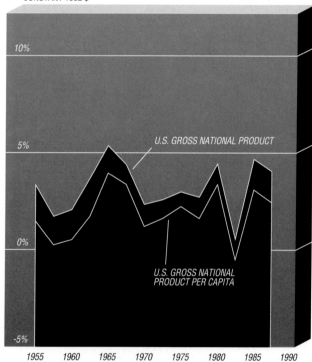

Source: Economic Report of the President, 1988

At a time of growing global economic integration, the nation's international economic position has turned for the worse.
Since 1981, the U.S. international trade balance has moved from
a net surplus (current account) of $6.9 billion to a $160 billion
deficit six years later (Figure 2.12). This negative balance reflects
both strong demand by U.S. consumers for imported goods and
a decline in the U.S. export volume—most pronounced for
manufactured products, including high tech products (an area of
traditional strength for the United States). This sustained trade
imbalance and the parallel growth of the federal budget deficit
have stimulated major inflows of foreign assets (Figure 2.13),
which in turn have led to an unprecedented development: the
United States has shifted from the position of a net international
creditor in 1982 (with around $150 billion in foreign assets) to
that of a net debtor nation in 1986 (with around $263 billion of
foreign debt) and the prospect of the debt increasing to $500
billion (or more) by 1990.

ANNUAL CHANGE. 4 YEAR MOVING AVERAGE
CONSTANT 1982 $

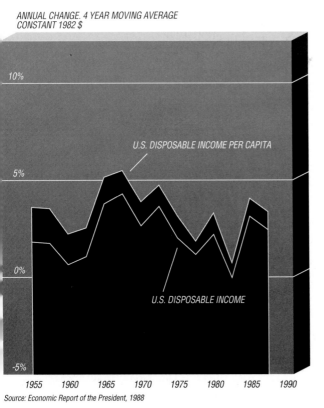

10%

U.S. DISPOSABLE INCOME PER CAPITA

5%

0%

U.S. DISPOSABLE INCOME

-5%

1955   1960   1965   1970   1975   1980   1985   1990

Source: Economic Report of the President, 1988

FIGURE 2.8
**TRENDS
IN GROWTH
OF INCOME**

The expansion of the recent business cycle notwithstanding, real growth in income has, at best, stagnated since the early 1970s. As depicted in Figure 2.14, median family income (in constant dollars) is still marginally lower now than in 1973, having sustained several years of decline since that time. The median income for males working full time is presently well below the level of 1973, and has generally declined since then. Indeed, it is only the rise in income from sources other than labor (i.e., interest and transfer payments) and the emergence of two-paycheck households that have masked a decline in real wages.

In this respect, the primary villain has been the nation's trouble with labor productivity from the mid-1960s through the early 1980s, particularly when compared with earlier periods and other nations during those same years. Records indicate that over the past 15 years, the U.S. economy has grown primarily through expansion of the population and the labor force rather than through improved productivity.

Evidence of renewed growth in labor productivity among

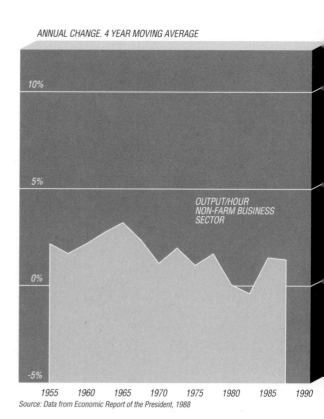

FIGURE 2.9
TREND IN GROWTH OF U.S. PRODUCTIVITY

ANNUAL CHANGE. 4 YEAR MOVING AVERAGE

10%

5%

OUTPUT/HOUR
NON-FARM BUSINESS
SECTOR

0%

-5%

1955   1960   1965   1970   1975   1980   1985   1990

Source: Data from Economic Report of the President, 1988

ome industries now provides grounds for optimism. As shown
a Table 2.1, such important economic sectors as manufacturing
nd trade have reversed the downward trends and shown signifi-
ant productivity-based growth in the last several years. On the
ther hand, several service sectors—industry groupings of in-
reasing importance to the economy because of their job-
reating potential—still remain well below productivity growth
ates established in the 1950s and 1960s.

Also notable are the growing competitive hurdles that U.S.
usinesses have encountered in both domestic and international
narkets. Numerous factors have contributed to this problem,
ncluding the burden of an overvalued dollar. Many economists
lso point to domestic factors that have hamstrung American
irms' ability to compete. One such cause is the country's low rate
of government investment in the national infrastructure. An-
ther is lagging capital investment by the nation's businesses
ompared with other developed countries—Figures 2.15 and
.16 provide illuminating long-run international comparisons.

Sector	1986 output share (percent)	1948 to 1973	1973 to 1981	1981 to 1986
GOODS-PRODUCING				
Farm	2.6	4.6	5.2	6.4
Mining	4.0	4.0	-6.8	4.8
Construction	5.7	.6	-2.7	-1.1
Manufacturing	27.3	2.8	1.3	4.5
Durable manufacturing	17.4	2.4	1.1	6.0
Nondurable manufacturing	9.9	3.4	1.7	2.1
SERVICE-PRODUCING:				
Transportation	4.3	2.3	-.2	.7
Communication	3.2	5.2	4.3	3.8
Utilities	3.5	5.9	.4	1.2
Trade	21.7	2.7	.5	3.0
Wholesale	9.5	3.1	-.1	4.0
Retail	12.2	2.4	.5	2.5
Finance, insurance, and real estate	11.0	1.4	-.4	-.3
Services	15.4	2.2	.3	-.1
Government enterprises	1.5	-.1	1.2	-.8
BUSINESS	100.0	2.9	.6	1.7

TABLE 2.1
PRODUCTIVITY GROWTH BY INDUSTRY SECTOR

MEASURED AS ANNUAL GROWTH IN REAL VALUE ADDED PER HOUR PAID (Average annual percent change, except as noted)

Source: Economic Report of the President, 1988.

The nation's relatively high cost of capital and its propensity to consume rather than to save also have contributed to the problem. Other postulated causes include the country's reluctance to invest adequately in private sector research and development, difficulties in adopting production innovations, lagging attention to quality control and a declining level of educational achievement in public schools.

And, as the 21st century nears, the aging population will impose greater burdens upon working-age groups. The recent debate over Social Security and Medicare is but a precursor of this intergenerational issue. Fortunately, the United States will not be the first among the industrialized nations to cope with a "top-heavy" population. Japan and several Western European countries also will face this problem in the near future.

Thus, despite the buoyancy of the present expansion, a constellation of problems will challenge the nation and its leaders.

FIGURE 2.10
INTERNATIONAL COMPARISONS

AVERAGE REAL GROWTH RATES IN GROSS NATIONAL PRODUCT

AVERAGE ANNUAL RATE OF GROWTH

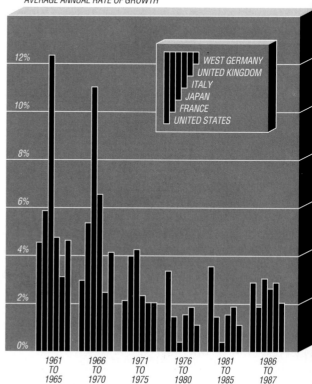

WEST GERMANY
UNITED KINGDOM
ITALY
JAPAN
FRANCE
UNITED STATES

Source: Data from Economic Report of the President, 1988.

GDP PER CAPITA, THOUSAND DOLLARS

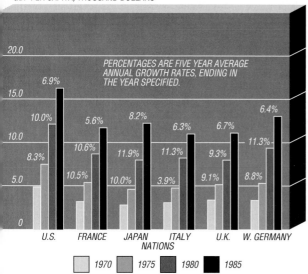

20.0

PERCENTAGES ARE FIVE YEAR AVERAGE
ANNUAL GROWTH RATES, ENDING IN
THE YEAR SPECIFIED.

6.9%

15.0

10.0%   5.6%   8.2%   6.4%

                        6.3%   6.7%

10.0

8.3%   10.6%   11.9%   11.3%   9.3%   11.3%

5.0   10.5%   10.0%   3.9%   9.1%   8.8%

0

U.S.   FRANCE   JAPAN   ITALY   U.K.   W. GERMANY
NATIONS

1970   1975   1980   1985

ource: Statistical Abstracts of the U.S., 1988 (GDP calculated based on purchasing power
arties to facilitate cross national comparisons)

FIGURE 2.11
**INTERNATIONAL
COMPARISONS**

GROWTH IN
GROSS DOMESTIC
PRODUCT PER
CAPITA

U.S. AND
SELECTED OTHER
INDUSTRIALIZED
NATIONS

BILLIONS OF DOLLARS (CURRENT)

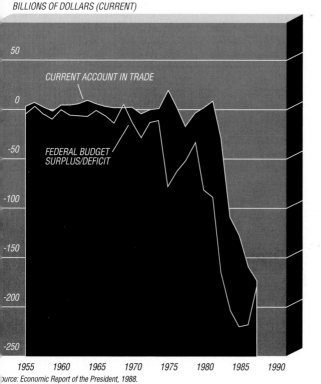

50

CURRENT ACCOUNT IN TRADE

0

-50   FEDERAL BUDGET
SURPLUS/DEFICIT

-100

-150

-200

-250

1955   1960   1965   1970   1975   1980   1985   1990
ource: Economic Report of the President, 1988.

FIGURE 2.12
**BALANCES
IN TRADE
AND
THE FEDERAL
BUDGET**

in the 1990s—the federal budget deficit, imbalances in interna
tional trade and finance (and the risks involved in resolving thes
imbalances), lagging productivity in important industries an
domestic obstacles to improving industry's ability to compete
The rate of progress toward resolving these challenges in th
1990s will, of course, influence the nation's unfolding economi
opportunities as it enters the 21st century.

THE FUTURE OF ECONOMIC GROWTH

While these challenges will create the agenda for futur
policies and business leadership, certain external forces will b
critical in shaping the nation's economic development. These ar
the continuing thrust toward global economic integration, th
adoption of advanced technology, the increasing rigors of busi
ness competition and long-run structural changes in the compo
sition of the economy.

FIGURE 2.13
COMPONENTS OF THE SAVING-INVESTMENT BALANCE

PERCENT OF GNP

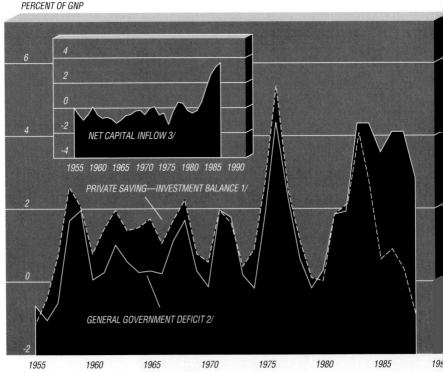

1/ Gross private savings minus gross private domestic investment.
2/ Federal, State, and local deficit.
3/ Defined as net foreign saving.
Note—Data for 1987 are preliminary.
Source: Economic Report of the President, 1988.

CONTINUING INTEGRATION OF THE
INTERNATIONAL ECONOMIC SYSTEM

One of the most important developments of the postwar period has been the interdependence of the world's economies. The pace of this integration has quickened in recent years, with the effect that markets for goods, services, technology, labor and money are now essentially global. This unprecedented transformation of the world's economic system is now well established. But the next 25 years—and particularly the next 10—should witness a deepening of the effects and implications for all major countries.

The volume of world trade in goods and services has expanded dramatically in the past several decades. Capabilities for globally competitive production, marketing and distribution have become a prerequisite for any successful business in the principal industrial countries. Consumers, in their search for value and quality, are demonstrating a growing willingness to purchase the products and services of foreign nations.

MEDIAN ANNUAL INCOMES PER THOUSAND 1986 $

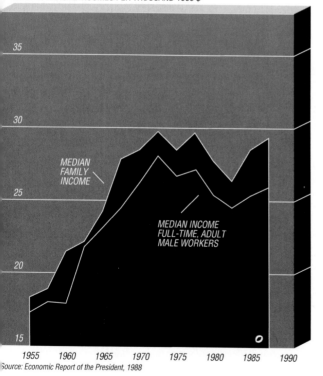

FIGURE 2.14
**TRENDS
IN INCOME**

MEDIAN
FAMILY
INCOME

MEDIAN INCOME
FULL-TIME, ADULT
MALE WORKERS

Source: Economic Report of the President, 1988

Advanced technological skills, once the province of nation with long-standing scientific histories (the United States, Ge many, France, the United Kingdom), are spreading throughou the world, especially to newly industrialized nations such Brazil and South Korea, and new industrial competitors such Singapore, Taiwan and Hong Kong. Multinational corporation have become an important force in spreading technology. Labo also has begun to move more freely, even between continent Money and securities are traded around the world, largely on 24-hour basis and in volumes that often exceed the value of goo and services traded. Aided by sophisticated global communic tions systems and always seeking out new opportunities, aggre sive international financial organizations can penetrate nearly al market.

In the United States, as noted in the 1985 report of th President's Commission on Industrial Competitiveness, a tru domestic economy has ceased to exist. Some 70 percent of th goods produced by the nation's businesses now compete direct with goods produced abroad: an estimated 20 percent of U. manufacturing is exported. Imports and exports each amount around 10 percent of GNP, compared with only 6 percent in th mid-1960s.

This economic integration can be expected to deepen over th next several decades. Globalization will provide new markets f U.S. firms. But more nations will be producing the goods ar services desired by the world's consumers. The pace of glob technology transfer will quicken. In the absence of new barrie to trade, large enterprises, wherever they may be headquartere will seek outlets in the internationalized marketplace. With th impetus, the volume of world trade will grow rapidly; exports ar imports will gain a greater share and greater influence on th economies of the trading nations.

An important side effect of this interdependence will be th nation's loss of sovereignty over its economic affairs. The grov ing importance of imports and exports in the national balance accounts and the international flow of money—with accompan ing flexible exchange rates and comparatively liberal trade a rangements—means that any nation's prospects will be heavi influenced by the economic strength and policies of other maj nations. For instance, the economic policies pursued by th Federal Republic of Germany affect interest rates U.S. consume pay for loans; a business slowdown in Japan sends ripples arour the world; and consumer behavior in the United States dete mines corporate investment decisions in France and the Unit Kingdom. Indeed, one of the major challenges of the next sever decades will be how successfully the world's economic powe an coordinate their economic policies and aspirations to mutual advantage.

Applying Advanced Technology. Scientific advances and technological innovations have been particularly powerful influences upon U.S. economic development in the second half of this century. During the 1950s and 1960s, leading-edge competence in science and engineering contributed to the country's overwhelming competitive advantage over other nations. Technological prowess promises to be equally if not more influential over the next 25 years.

Table 2.2 lists a number of major areas in which new technology is expected to have significant effects on the U.S. economy through the end of this century and, importantly, on the economies of other major nations as well. Each represents the commercialization of technical capabilities for which the basic groundwork has been laid largely by recent scientific achievements.

Materials science, through progress over several decades, has

PERCENT GROWTH OF LABOR PRODUCTIVITY

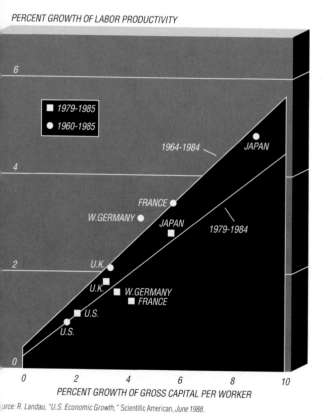

FIGURE 2.15
INTERNATIONAL COMPARISONS

GROWTH IN LABOR PRODUCTIVITY VS. GROWTH IN CAPITAL

■ 1979-1985
● 1960-1985

1964-1984 — JAPAN

FRANCE ●
W.GERMANY ●   JAPAN ■   1979-1984

U.K. ●
U.K. ■
■ W.GERMANY
■ FRANCE
■ U.S.
U.S. ●

PERCENT GROWTH OF GROSS CAPITAL PER WORKER

Source: R. Landau, "U.S. Economic Growth," Scientific American, June 1988.

120858

gained the ability to engineer the production of a range materials with unique and customized properties (e.g., strengt durability, cost, conductance, resistance to degradants) for sp cific products and processes. Major classes of materials develop from this research, such as high-performance ceramics (includir materials with high-temperature superconductive propertie advanced polymers and nonmetallic composites already ha become essential elements in advancing microelectronics, info mation technologies and aerospace. And over the next decad advanced materials of many kinds are expected to replace conve tional metals and other natural materials in a widening scope products—airplanes, automobiles, buildings and appliances.

Materials with unique properties—electronic, conductiv acoustic—will provide the basis for developing radically ne capabilities, as illustrated by what silicon and gallium arseni have done for computers and communications. Superconductir

FIGURE 2.16
INTERNATIONAL COMPARISONS

GROSS DOMESTIC PRODUCT GROWTH VS. RATE OF SAVINGS

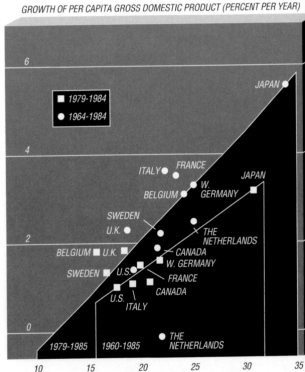

GROWTH OF PER CAPITA GROSS DOMESTIC PRODUCT (PERCENT PER YEAR)

AVERAGE RATIO OF GROSS SAVINGS TO GROSS DOMESTIC PRODUCT (PERCEN

Source: R. Landau, "U.S. Economic Growth," Scientific American, June 1988.

materials represent one such area with considerable potential for technologies utilizing magnetic and electrical energies, though much basic scientific work remains and it still is unclear whether there will be significant commercial applications before the year 2000.

The microelectronics revolution began in the 1950s and has continued to yield a host of electrically driven devices with applications in cognitive and sensing functions, command and control and communications. This area of technology will continue to grow, with the commercialization of more sophisticated devices for the private sector (e.g., automated controls for process operations, sensing devices with enhanced powers), for defense (e.g., devices for command and control, communications) and for households (consumer products for audio and video components, and household appliance management). Some of these developments will be new generations of existing devices—with improved speed and performance, further miniaturization and such added capabilities as increased cognition and decision functions. A fertile area for development with important commercial implications over the next decade will be optoelectronics, the blending of optical fibers and lightwave processing.

The revolution in computing, information processing and

ADVANCED MATERIALS
   High performance structural and electronic ceramics, polymer and metal matrix composites, rapid solidification metals, advanced surfaces and interfaces, membranes.

ELECTRONICS
   Advanced microelectronics (improved speed, performance, size, and capabilities), optoelectronics (Optical fiber and light wave processing), millimeter wave technology (substituting for and freeing up existing radio frequency systems).

AUTOMATION
   Computer integrated/flexible systems with manufacturing applications (CAD/CAM, robotics), business/office computers (high efficiency technologies for information storage, retrieval, and exchange), technical services computers (high volume information storage, retrieval, exchange).

BIOTECHNOLOGY
   Design/production of highly selective bioactive compounds through genetic engineering, improved control of chemical processes through bioprocessing.

COMPUTING
   Advanced computing equipment (supercomputers, parallel processing, advanced architectures), artificial intelligence (expert systems, natural language processing, robotics).

MEDICINE
   Improved drugs, advanced instruments and devices (e.g., NMR imaging, CAT scanning, radiation treatments).

Source: U.S. Department of Commerce, 1987achievements.

TABLE 2.2
AREAS OF NEW TECHNOLOGY WITH MAJOR ECONOMIC IMPACT 1988-2000

communications will continue. For most businesses and house
holds, the thrust of this technology will be primarily in the form
of faster computer and communications equipment with greate
memory capability, continuing reduction in hardware costs
wider range of software and expanding on-line information
resources.

Advanced information and communications technology wil
continue to expand its applications across industry and com
merce. In industrial plants, integrated operations based on
computer control—through technologies such as computer
aided design, robotics, computer-controlled machine tools—
will provide increased automation and flexibility in plant opera
tions. In business, improved computer capabilities (for high
efficiency information storage, retrieval and exchange) and infor
mation transmission (local and long-distance integrated net
works) will expand. In businesses providing technical services
computers will be enhanced for high-volume storage, retrieva
and exchange. A particularly important communications devel
opment certain to affect all sectors will be the increasing spread
of optical cable lines capable of integrating the transmission of
audio, video and data signals in the United States and worldwide

Over the next decade, the frontiers in computer engineering
will be supercomputer development, further miniaturization
advanced operations (e.g., parallel processing, other new archi
tectures), computer emulation of cognitive and decision proc
esses and the development of software for these new capabilities
One practical development from these activities will be the
availability of a wider spectrum of expert systems and other
artificial intelligence devices for widespread application in the
economy.

Advances in molecular biology, genetics and biochemistry
have greatly enhanced the understanding of applying living
systems to the production of refined materials and products. The
next decade promises to integrate these capabilities into the
economy through techniques such as recombinant DNA, gene
transfer, embryo manipulation and transfer, cell cultures, plan
regeneration, monoclonal antibodies and bioprocess engineer
ing. For the near term, the greatest impacts will be therapeutic
drugs, treatments and medical diagnostics, where a growing
"toolbox" of DNA probes, antibody binders and the like wil
provide vast new resources for biomedical measurements. Also
emerging will be specialty chemicals at higher levels of purity and
improved costs; agricultural chemicals, particularly new animal
vaccines, microbials and growth stimulants; and bioprocessing
for improved control and lower costs in chemical synthesis. The
ability to engineer the genetic materials of plants and simple

rganisms to achieve desired properties, for instance, plants ith improved resistance to weather and pests, microbes able to ach and concentrate rare metals and microbes to digest pollut- nts, will be a longer-term achievement of this fast-developing eld.

Medicine also will witness important developments over the ext decade. A major development will be the refinement and read of non-invasive diagnostic tools based on electronic nsing techniques, such as nuclear magnetic resonance imaging, omputerized, axial tomography and miniature probes.

Identifying technologies with high economic impact beyond ae year 2000 is difficult and more speculative. Scientific break- aroughs in the next decade undoubtedly will contribute to the chnological priorities of the new century. It is reasonable to xpect that the major developmental areas of the 1990s— dvanced materials, electronics, automation, biotechnology, omputers, medicine—will continue to play an important role in ostering economic growth and creating jobs. None of these reas will have run their full course, either in terms of the intrinsic apabilities of the technologies or their penetration into the conomy. Each can be expected to yield further generations of efinements and new applications. Other fields in which emerg- ag technical and scientific capabilities may yield important ontributions to the economy beyond the year 2000 include: the se of space for industrial production, the commercialization of roducts utilizing superconducting properties in new materials nd internal combustion engines assembled from advanced eramics.

By the year 2000 and beyond, energy technologies also will ontribute to the environmental and efficiency needs of a grow- ag economy. Considerable progress is being made in the field of hotovoltaics. New materials and advanced designs are proving he basis for solar cells with much higher conversion efficiencies han just a few years ago. While further development is needed, his technology now is becoming a competitive source of electric- ty generation in special situations. A number of advanced "clean oal" technologies—fluidized beds, combined cycle gasifica- ion—are being readied for wide applications as the nation looks oward a new cycle of capacity expansion to meet future needs. Nuclear power can be expected to expand through a new eneration of self-controlling, advanced technology fission plants. The post-2000 period may well witness major progress in fusion ower or capabilities to extract economically and deliver to narket the vast energy potential of "unconventional" natural gas leposits (in coal seams, Devonian shale, tight sands and geopres- urized zones).

ESCALATING COMPETITION AND INTENSIFYING PRODUCT CYCLES

Intensifying competition has been an important and growin force with which U.S. businesses and the nation as a whole hav had to contend in recent years. The future promises no respite Indeed, competition seems likely to amplify in the years aheac

By the late 1960s, the United States had achieved an ove whelming advantage over other nations in technological skil and the ability to develop and commercialize new products an processes rapidly. Based on this technological and organization lead, the United States primed the world's engine of economi growth well into the 1970s.

But over the past 15 years this advantage has been erodec Japan, major European nations and the rapidly growing indus trial economies of Southeast Asia are challenging this country performance record. To some extent, the challenge was expecte as the old barriers to the free flow of scientific and technic information were lowered and the wounds inflicted by Worl War II healed. Economic necessity, improving levels of educa tion, stabler political systems and the global spread of technolog have endowed a growing number of nations—including som with wage levels well below this country's—with the manageria financial and technical ability to compete successfully in U.S markets.

At the same time, U.S. firms have encountered difficulties i commercializing new products for increasingly discriminatin world markets. Today's product cycle often begins with Japa introducing a new product that U.S. firms then emulate, perhap with a time lag.

Why is this happening? Numerous reasons have been offerec Nations such as Japan and the Federal Republic of Germany no spend a substantially larger fraction of their GNP on nondefens research and development than the United States. At the sam time, U.S. government support of university research has de clined dramatically in real terms since the late 1960s. Anothe factor is the low levels of private investment in plant an equipment; in recent years the United States has reported th lowest rate per worker among all the major Western economi powers. This may be due to the high cost of capital and becaus U.S. business decisions typically have short-term horizons, un like those of the Japanese. Also contributing to the situation is th declining interest of U.S. college students in science and engi neering and the generally lower status accorded to engineerin and production jobs in U.S. businesses—conditions that do n prevail in the competitor countries. Finally, there is a widenin

erception that U.S. products are declining in quality, as con-
umers seem willing to pay a premium to obtain Japanese or
uropean goods.

These deficiencies—whether perceived or real—assume par-
cular importance for the future as faster product cycles, deepen-
g competition and managerial risk-taking on an international
ale become the order of the day. Market segmentation, increas-
g sophistication among the world's consumers, as well as the
sing force of competition are shortening and intensifying the
cle for many products. New product development, marketing
d distribution must occur rapidly as the window of opportunity
ecomes ever smaller before imitations appear in the market-
ace. Product obsolescence is accelerating, with overall innova-
on cycles of 3-5 years or even less becoming increasingly
equent. And typically, higher development costs associated
ith these cycles escalate the financial risks of innovation.

Another important development is the likely expansion of the
ope of economic competition. Economic competition by other
ations generally has been centered around tangible goods.
ompetition in providing services—banking and finance, engi-
eering, design, communications, information processing and
anagement, health care, education—has been, by contrast,
uch less intensive. Indeed, despite little evidence of significant
roductivity growth, U.S. service firms have continued to domi-
ate these areas both domestically and internationally.

Ongoing trends, however, portend important changes. Inter-
ational barriers to providing services across national boundaries
enerally are falling; both governments and businesses are begin-
ing to accept bids from international firms for specialized
ervices. Advances in computers and telecommunications and
heir worldwide application make it vastly easier for financial
rms, banks, accountants, advertisers and others to expand their
lobal operations. Further, many services are becoming more
eeply embedded in the production of goods. Services such as
roduct and market research, transportation, retailing and adver-
ising account for a growing share of the value added in manu-
actured products. Future trends in competitive and product
ycles promise to deepen this effect. Studies also indicate that
nnovations in organization and technology can provide a risk-
aking enterprise the competitive edge in the service sector. And
ince differences in labor costs continue to prevail around the
vorld, competition from the younger industrial nations will
egin to strike the service sector of the more mature economies
f North America and Europe.

Shifts in the Composition of the Economy. Most mature
ndustrial nations, such as the United States and Japan, will

undergo noteworthy shifts in the structural composition of their economies over the long run. Primary industries such as agricul ture and resource extraction (mining, oil and gas exploration will continue to decline as a share of the total economy.

In manufacturing the emphasis shifts. Over the mid-term manufacturing moves from low value-added/high-volume sec tors that are extensively dependent on raw materials, standard ized production and labor costs (e.g., primary metals, some non durable goods) to high value-added/low-to-moderate volum sectors where flexible batch production allows product customi zation (e.g., computers, instruments). Over the long run, growth will be concentrated in industries involved in information prod ucts. Service sectors—education, wholesale and retail trade information management for businesses—become more domi nant in creating value in the economy because they contribute

FIGURE 2.17
U.S. TRENDS IN OUTPUT COMPOSITION

SHARE OF TOTAL U.S. GNP

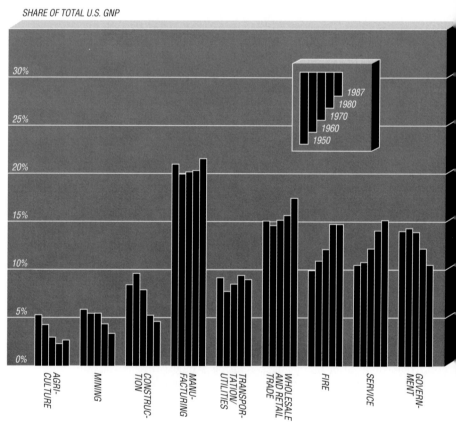

Source: Economic Report of the President, 1988.

arger share to total output and also add value to goods through
design, market research and advertising. Much attention has been
paid to the growth of service industries and the prospect that the
United States will become primarily a services-dominated economy. Statistics tracing the composition of the economy over the
past several decades, as summarized in Figures 2.17 and 2.18 for
the period since 1950, reveal important shifts. The emergence of
the services economy, however, is more persuasive from an
employment, and employment growth, perspective than from a
perspective of value of output. Indeed, manufacturing's ability
to maintain its share of total output has been one of the more
enduring features of the nation's economic structure.*

In 1950, goods-producing industries (agriculture, mining
and resource extraction, construction and manufacturing) accounted for 42 percent of GNP. Of these, manufacturing accounted for just under 22 percent of GNP. Service industries
(transportation and utilities, trade, finance and insurance, real
estate, services and government) accounted for around 58 percent of GNP. By 1987, the share of GNP accounted for by goods
production had declined to 33 percent; the share of the service
industries, on the other hand, had increased to more than 67
percent.

These changes in the composition of output reflect the
ascendancy of the services sectors in the economy. Notably,
though, the decline in the overall role of goods-producing
industries did not result primarily from a decline of manufacturing but rather from sharp declines in agriculture, mining, resource extraction and construction levels. To be sure, there have
been important changes in the makeup of manufacturing since
the 1940s—a declining role for non-durables and an increasing
one for durables (and, in that category, fewer books and kitchen
appliances and more motor vehicles and electronic equipment).
But its share of GNP has remained at 22 percent for some time.
The same general pattern emerges from an examination of the
composition of added value; manufacturing has contributed 19
to 23 percent of the total ever since the late 1940s.

The shifts in the composition of the economy are more
pronounced in employment. In 1950, goods-producing industries accounted for 52 percent of all jobs, the services industries
for 48 percent. By 1977, progressive declines in agricultural and

*Note: New questions are being raised in the academic community about the data series
assembled by the U.S. Department of Commerce to measure output and productivity in the
manufacturing sector. The concern is that problems of measurement (in manufacturing and in
other sectors) may be masking a significant post-1979 shrinkage in the manufacturing sector's
share of total output. Estimates of corrected measures suggest that the manufacturing sector's
share may have declined by as much as 3 to 4 percent since the 1970s, not increased by 1 percent
or so as the conventional statistics indicate. Nevertheless, the point about the sustained role of
manufacturing in the nation's economic output remains valid.

manufacturing employment (and virtual stability in the construction sector) had reduced the goods-producing industries' share of total employment to 27 percent (or almost half the 1950 share). By contrast, rapid and sustained employment growth in trade, finance and insurance, real estate, services and government has driven the service industries' share of total employment to more than 70 percent.

The growing importance of the service industries has generally carried through to new job creation. As illustrated in Table 2.3, of the 10.7 million jobs created outside the agricultural sector between 1975 and 1985, 29 percent were in trade and 39 percent in services; only 5 percent were in manufacturing and 8 percent in government. During 1955-1965, by contrast, manufacturing had accounted for 12 percent of the new jobs, trade for 22 percent, services for 28 percent and government for 32 percent.

Manufacturing will continue to lead the economy in share of

FIGURE 2.18
**U.S. TRENDS
IN EMPLOYMENT
COMPOSITION**

SHARE OF TOTAL U.S. EMPLOYMENT

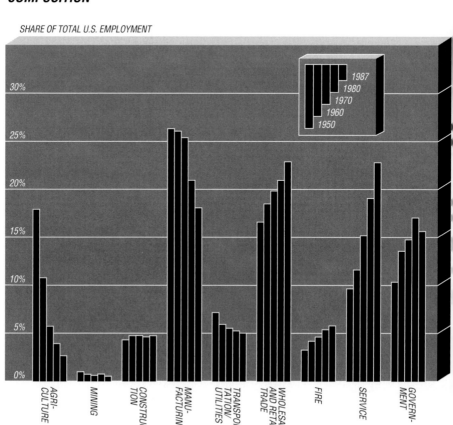

Source: Economic Report of the President, 1988.

total output and value added. The composition of the manufacturing sector, however, may change, with more growth in those segments that involve high-technology products, processes and considerable customization. Manufacturing will shift away from natural resource-based industries and toward advanced machinery, electronic products, computers, communications equipment, biotechnology and so on. While construction will maintain its share, agriculture and mining can be expected to play an ever smaller role in the national economy.

These trends reveal a national economy that, despite important shifts, remains strongly dependent on the production of tangible goods. But employment, particularly new jobs, is increasingly driven by the wide range of industries that provide services. These basic structural trends should continue over the next 25 years. The sectors that provide services to the domestic economy and to the world are likely to be the primary contributors to future growth in employment. If their comparatively slow pace of productivity improvement can be accelerated, these sectors' contributions to value added also may grow.

PROSPECTS FOR GROWTH

The 1990s will be a period of considerable challenge and risk for the economy. It promises, though, to be a period when the U.S. economy re-establishes a new base for growth. Adjustments will be necessary. Change will be demanded by the new realities of the global economy, the changing mix of U.S. output and employment, growing international competition in many markets, the harnessing of the nation's federal budget deficit and international financial imbalances and the significantly slower growth rates of the population and the labor force. Problems appear manageable, provided "wild card" developments (e.g.,

Sector	Period 1955-1965	1965-1975	1975-1985
Manufacturing	11.9	1.9	4.8
Mining and construction	2.0	2.5	6.3
Transportation and utilities	-1.0	3.1	3.4
Wholesale and retail trade	21.8	26.5	29.0
Finance, insurance, and real estate	6.9	7.4	8.7
Services	27.7	30.2	39.1
Government	31.7	28.4	8.2

TABLE 2.3
SECTORAL COMPOSITION OF NEW JOBS IN THE U.S. ECONOMY

NOTE: There were 10.1 million new jobs created during 1955-1965, 16.2 million during 1965-1975, and 20.7 during 1975-1985. Percentages may not total 100 due to rounding.

Source: National Academy of Science, 1987.

new energy supply dislocations or uncontrolled world financial swings) can be avoided through a more peaceful and cooperative world community.

Prospects for economic growth, as the 21st century begins will be influenced by how well the nation navigates the shoals of the 1990s. Much rests on the country's ability to sustain growth in productivity through technology, better organization, a higher savings rate and a national will to succeed. Beyond the year 2000, further slowing of population growth and a barely expanding labor force will make progress more difficult. Further, when the baby boom generation is ready to retire after 2010, and in large numbers by 2020, public policy will be put to the test to balance needs, available resources and issues of intergenerational equity.

A common policy theme for the 1990s and the 21st century is that real economic growth will depend increasingly on productivity growth. This is because the labor force probably will grow more slowly. Thus, in laying the groundwork for improving productivity, the country must reverse the downward trends that have characterized much of the most recent 15 years. This improvement will have to be achieved at a time when the economy will become more dependent on service industries— segments of the economy that in recent years have exhibited a relatively low growth in productivity.

What rate of economic growth can the nation expect to sustain in the future? Many uncertainties prevail, including the precise rate of labor force growth, the speed of structural change in the economy, the degree to which productivity is improved and the extent of business sensitivity to global economic conditions.

While many outcomes are possible, a rough estimate of the potential for real GNP growth can be fashioned by adding estimates of labor force growth and the rate of improvement in total labor productivity. The future trend in either of these factors is certainly subject to uncertainty. But working ranges and the results of varying combinations can be estimated for each.

The rate at which the labor force is likely to increase depends on the growth rate of the working-age population and the extent to which this population participates in the labor force. Current forecasts of the U.S. population prepared by the Census Bureau (see Figure 2.1) and estimates of participation rates (based on historical trends) provide a working range. For the 1990s, labor force growth could range from 0.6 percent to 1.4 percent annually, with a mid-range rate of 1.2 percent (based on the Bureau's middle series projection). From 2000 to 2015, the range lies between 0.3 and 1.2 percent, with a mid-range estimate of 0.7 percent (based, again, on the middle series projection).

What about the rate at which overall labor productivity will improve? This simple and frequently used aggregate ratio of the value of economic output divided by the hours of work reflects complex interaction among capital investment, technology, the quality of the labor force, the composition of the economy and the nature of labor-management relationships. As noted earlier, labor productivity has rebounded in the United States over the past five years, averaging a growth rate of around 1.5 percent since late 1982 (based on solid gains by manufacturing and trade, but on continuing weakness in finance/insurance/real estate and services). Throughout the late 1970s and early 1980s, by comparison, labor productivity improved by only 0.8 percent annually on average.

For the 1990s, a working range of total labor productivity improvement spans 0.8 percent annually on the pessimistic side (i.e., a return to the conditions of the 1970s and early 1980s), 1.5 percent at mid-range (continuation of the present trend) and 2.0 percent on the optimistic side (consistent with current trends in the goods-producing industry sectors and a resumption of past rates of improvement in the service sectors). Estimates for 2000 to 2015 are even more speculative, but growth rates similar to those expected for the 1990s provide a useful forecast range. If new technology, investment in productive resources, the development of a highly skilled and motivated work force and a strong commitment to global competitiveness combine in the right way, U.S. productivity improvements in the post-2000 period could occur ever faster.

The assumptions set forth above produce a range of possible outcomes for future economic growth as shown in Table 2.4. What emerges for the 1990s is a potential real GNP growth rate ranging from 1.4 to 3.4 percent annually, with a mid-range expectation of 2.7 percent (i.e., a combination of the mid-assumptions for both labor force and productivity growth). Similarly, for the 2000 to 2015 period, the range is 1.1 to 3.2 percent, with a mid-range figure of 2.2 percent.

While these figures provide a sense of the range of possibilities, they are simplified quantification of complex events. Numerous uncertainties surround some of the key variables that will shape the course of the economy.

PATTERNS OF LIFE: INDUSTRY, COMMERCE AND HOUSEHOLDS

THE CHANGING ORGANIZATION OF BUSINESS

The growing complexity of the business environment—marked by globalization, greater sophistication and specialization of customers' needs, more capable competitors, the intensification of product cycles—is escalating the demands for managers and entrepreneurs. U.S. manufacturing firms have felt these pressures acutely for the past decade. While U.S. service firms have generally not been as severely buffeted (with those in areas such as accounting, engineering design, law, communications and international finance continuing to enjoy strong global positions), signs point to similar pressures on their performance in the years ahead.

The specifics of business competition and performance requirements vary widely across U.S. industry and commerce. Even so, the broad outline of what "being competitive" means for the mainstream of U.S. businesses is apparent in current trends:

- Organizational agility in defining a need, designing a product and completing full-scale production in months rather than years.
- Capability to customize products efficiently and to analyze customer requirements; increasing specialization of customer needs so that markets take on more "niche"

TABLE 2.4

THE POTENTIAL FOR U.S. GNP GROWTH OVER THE NEXT 25 YEARS

	The 1990s LABOR PRODUCTIVITY GROWTH Average Annual Percent Change		
	Pessimistic (0.8)	Mid (1.5)	Optimistic (2.0)
LABOR FORCE GROWTH Average Annual Percent Change			
Low (0.6)	1.4	2.1	2.6
Mid (1.2)	2.0	2.7	3.2
High (1.4)	2.2	2.9	3.4

	2000 TO 2015 LABOR PRODUCTIVITY GROWTH Average Annual Percent Change		
	Pessimistic (0.8)	Mid (1.5)	Optimistic (2.0)
LABOR FORCE GROWTH Average Annual Percent Change			
Low (0.3)	1.1	1.8	2.3
Mid (0.7)	1.5	2.2	2.7
High (1.2)	2.0	2.7	3.2

NOTES:
1. Figures are estimates of future GNP growth (average annual rates) given the corresponding labor force and labor productivity assumptions.
2. Alternative assumptions regarding rates of future labor force growth are based on current Bureau of the Census population forecasts (the low, middle, and high series projections).
3. Alternative assumptions for the rate of labor productivity improvement are based on U.S. historical experiences from 1950 through 1987 (see text).

qualities while remaining cost competitive.

- Rapid delivery and distribution of products over days instead of weeks or months.
- Close oversight of product quality and costs to deal with competitors who seek a share of the market.

These emerging requirements promise to stimulate changes and innovations in ways business management and production activities are organized.

Structure and Management. Many businesses, particularly medium and large size, will restructure to improve flexibility and agility under rapidly changing market conditions and to increase capabilities for product innovations and operational efficiency. The future workplace will be less hierarchical and more horizontal in structure, with more decentralized responsibility and greater initiative expected from units organized for individual projects. In short, it will emulate many characteristics of entrepreneurial small businesses.

This coming change is captured by management expert Peter Drucker. According to Drucker, these are the major implications of structural change:

The typical business organization 20 years hence will have fewer than half the levels of management of its counterpart today...(it) will be knowledge based, an organization composed largely of specialists who direct and discipline their own performance through organized feedback from colleagues, customers, and headquarters...The information-based organization requires far more specialists overall than the command-and-control companies we are accustomed to. Moreover, the specialists are found in operations, not at corporate headquarters...Traditional departments will serve as guardians of standards, as centers for training and the assignment of specialists. They won't be where the work gets done; that will happen largely in task-focused groups (*Harvard Business Review*, January/February, 1988).

Manufacturing and the Factory of the Future. The experience of successful manufacturing firms, particularly Japanese corporations, over the past decade has demonstrated that a powerful competitive edge can be forged through careful attention to efficient production processes and aggressive process innovation. Over the next decade and beyond, manufacturing will be remade in light of these experiences and the innovations that arise from them.

Advanced technology and improved management practices will be essential elements of this transformation. Table 2.5 summarizes a number of advanced processes expected to find applications in the manufacturing plants of the future. Many of these reflect increased automation, advanced resources for design and specialized production, reduced direct labor and greater control over product quality and the cost of plant operation. As Jack Meredith has observed in commenting on emerging trends and opportunities in manufacturing, "The factory of the future will be smaller than today's factory, closer to its customers (both literally and figuratively), more responsive and efficient, and will employ considerably fewer people." (*California Management Review*, Spring, 1987).

Transforming a firm's manufacturing capabilities can be both costly and organizationally painful. Therefore, advanced manufacturing processes will spread only gradually across the U.S. economy. Organizational innovations such as cellular production, immediate scheduling of inventory, the use of quality teams and systematic classification and coding of parts will come more easily because they are comparatively painless to adopt and can provide a substantial boost to factory productivity on their own. Over the long run, however, advanced technologies for extensive automation will play an even greater role, as their application becomes essential in achieving the levels of performance required by the new business environment.

Improving Productivity in Services. Improving productivity in services sectors will be difficult as indicated by the comparatively low productivity improvement in this part of the economy in the past 15 years. A closer look at recent trends and em-erging opportunities, however, supports an optimistic outlook.

In the past five years, important sectors such as communications and wholesale/retail trade have exhibited comparatively high levels of productivity growth. Also, numerous service businesses have been able to capitalize creatively on automated technologies, expanded scale (size of markets, access to financial resources and volume discounts, etc.) and product standardization. Examples of this include the displacement of small mom-and-pop grocers by large, high volume, bar-code checkout stores; the displacement of cook-to-order kitchens by fast-food franchises with their limited menus, production-line kitchens and automated registers; and the growth of national and international overnight mail and package delivery firms utilizing extensive automation of sorting and tracking systems. Further, electronic systems for collecting, analyzing and disseminating information and for speeding transactions have become major forces in wholesale and retail activities, engineering design, financial services, travel and entertainment.

Clearly, advanced technology and innovation in organization and management are widely applicable to the requirements of service businesses (as for manufacturing), and can provide significant improvements in productivity. Obviously, the larger companies, with significant capital-raising ability and technical sophistication, will find it easier to adopt new techniques. But the trend toward lower prices, greater modularity and improved versatility of automated equipment also should enable the smaller service companies to compete in large markets. Overall, the primary need is to link new technology and management techniques with market opportunities (whether domestic or global in scale). Table 2.6 provides illustrative examples of future directions for the services sector of the U.S. economy.

THE JOBS OF THE FUTURE

The occupational requirements of the industrial and commercial sectors change over time, as technological innovation, new

---

ENGINEERING
— *Computer-aided design (drafting, data searches, design modifications)*
— *Computer-aided engineering analysis (stress analysis, force and column loadings, etc.)*
— *Computer-aided process planning (automated generation of shop production operations and routings)*
— *Group technology classification/coding (classification of parts into families for enhanced engineering analysis and design)*

MANUFACTURING
— *Robots and numerically controlled tools*
— *Computer-aided manufacturing (automated manufacturing of parts and products by automated machining)*
— *Flexible manufacturing systems (multiple machining/turning centers with automated and computer-controlled material movements between centers; utilizing automated guided vehicle systems and automotive storage and retrieval systems)*
— *Cellular manufacturing (production of a part or product within one cell of mixed machines to eliminate extensive routing)*
— *Group technology classification/coding (use of parts families for efficient routing and retrieval)*
— *Advanced machining tools (reprogrammable lasers, water jets, electro-discharge machining)*
— *"Touch" setups (systems allowing very rapid machine and program changeovers for producing new products)*

MANAGEMENT
— *Just-in-time production, zero inventories (for improving the efficiencies of materials and parts flows throughout production, reduction of waste materials, reduction of costs from inventories)*
— *Computerized systems for manufacturing management (monitoring, bill of engineering materials, master scheduling, purchasing, cost accounting, etc.)*

TABLE 2.5
TECHNOLOGY AND PROCESSES FOR THE FACTORY OF THE FUTURE

Source: J.R. Meredith, "The Strategic Advantages of the Factory of the Future," California Management Review, Spring, 1987.

products, competition and public policy create needs for people with new skills. For the coming decade and into the next century, the needs for major realignments in the mix of occupations is evident. These changes will occur in response to new developments in business organization and work requirements that will be stimulated by the competitive imperative in a global economy.

According to the Hudson Institute's employment outlook in *Workforce 2000*, professional, technical, managerial, sales and business service jobs will have far better prospects than occupations traditionally required by manufacturing. Table 2.7, which provides a forecast of the rate at which various categories of jobs will grow to the year 2000, confirms the assessment that the demand for jobs that require special skills and a higher level of education and training (e.g., engineers, health professionals, computer and mathematical scientists) will grow more rapidly in the future.

In the past, the nation's economic growth was led by manufacturing that required skilled hands-on occupations such as craft

TABLE 2.6
OPPORTUNITIES FOR IMPROVING PRODUCTIVITY IN SERVICE INDUSTRIES

Illustrative Examples

- COMMUNICATIONS
  — *National/international distribution of video and audio materials through telecommunications technology for downloading onto home entertainment systems*
  — *Integrated electronic mail, facsimile, video/voice communications services for interoffice business communications*

- TRADE
  — *Rapid response inventory and distribution systems (including sales risk hedging capabilities)*
  — *"Buy direct from the manufacturer" sales systems based on cable TV advertising and personal computer accessible catalogues*
  — *Automated check-out counters in department stores*

- FINANCE, INSURANCE, REAL ESTATE
  — *Integrated real estate and mortgage options data bases/planning software accessible nationally through home computers*
  — *Consumer accessible data bases for identifying life insurance needs, evaluating product options and initiating applications*
  — *New banking and electronic funds transfer services through home computers*

- OTHER PRIVATE SERVICES
  — *Computerized classrooms for education*
  — *Automated self-diagnosis capabilities for routine health care clinics*
  — *Use of sophisticated robots to support routine nursing functions*
  — *Wider applications of remote sensing and monitoring systems in private security*

Source: The Hudson Institute, Workforce 2000, 1987; J. B. Quinn, et.al., "Technology in Services, " Scientific American, December 1987; and The Futures Group

workers, precision production workers and comparatively low-skilled laborers. The work force of the highly competitive, information-intensive and high-tech environment into which the country is moving will have a very different character.

Traditional hands-on workers and low-skilled laborers will be employed less and less. Demand will grow for technical professionals (twice as many may be needed by 2000 as in the mid-1980s), managers and support personnel (an increase of around 15 percent) and workers (as much as a third more) in sales and marketing. More than half of these jobs will require some education beyond the secondary level and almost a third will be filled by college graduates.

While low-paying jobs involving routine activities and low-skill requirements will not disappear, they will decline under the pressures of an advancing technology and the drive for more productivity. Occupations such as routine food preparation, farm work and personal service delivery are among the most vulnerable.

These occupational statistics address the quality of the future working environment—the levels of personal satisfaction and control afforded employees in their working life. The evolving economy may well generate more interesting and rewarding jobs, ranging from face-to-face sales positions to rewarding demands on technicians for the installation and repair of complex hardware and software technologies, and to opportunities for managers to build specialized teams with responsibilities for complex projects.

CHANGING HOUSEHOLD LIFESTYLES

National lifestyles are shaped by many forces, not the least of which are demographic and economic. Certainly, the number of households will be increasing faster than the population as a whole because of remarkable growth in the formation of nonfamily households. Longer life expectancy, a healthy elderly population, the survival of independently living widows, postponements of marriage in parallel with the social acceptance of cohabitation, frequent divorce and remarriage, increasing numbers of women in the labor force in and out of marriage—these and other factors explain why fewer than 15 percent of all households now fit the traditional pattern of a family with two children and only the husband working.

This diversity in living arrangements notwithstanding, American society is increasingly seen as preferring a stable household. Whether for purely economic reasons or because of women's rising economic aspirations, dual-earner households seem here to stay. They are likely to save less than the traditional families and to spend more on services and convenience goods so as to reduce the burden of domestic tasks for both breadwinners.

The next decade will see an even more pronounced trend towards sharing household tasks, including child-rearing. The current national debate over day care is illustrative of the pressures that two jobs impose on the modern household. Since these pressures are unlikely to abate, and as the cost of educating children continues to escalate and the burden of home ownership increases, American households will persist in seeking ways to ease their domestic responsibilities through technology in the home. They also will be placing new demands on employers for more flexible working conditions and fringe benefits for both partners.

TABLE 2.7
OCCUPATONAL TRENDS TO THE YEAR 2000

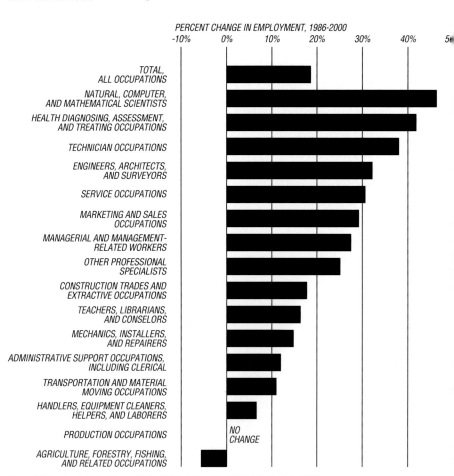

PERCENT CHANGE IN EMPLOYMENT, 1986-2000

Source: U.S. Department of Labor (Bureau of Labor Statistics), Occupational Outlook Handbook, April 1988.

As leisure time shrinks under the dual necessities of income earning and do-it-yourself home maintenance and improvement, householders will acquire more electronic and mechanical aids to help them cope with a faster pace of life. The value of time-saving equipment will rise as people place a premium on time for leisure and child-rearing.

Another phenomenon of modern American life is the convergence of urban and rural lifestyles. That convergence is brought about by economic changes in the agricultural sector, the rapid decline of the farm population, the suburbanization of the rural fringe of metropolitan areas, the location of urban-type employment centers in the countryside and the homogenizing effect of advertising and mass marketing. Also, dual-job holding to supplement farm income has created the same time pressures on the farm as on urban households.

With tensions between job and home responsibilities increasing, householders will seek additional adjustments in living and working patterns. These will include employment in the home as the old cottage industry concept is transformed into computer and telecommunications-assisted professional entrepreneurship or into "satellite" tasks reported into a central office. Another trend is household participation in the informal economy in which services are exchanged and goods produced that do not enter normal marketing channels. Such activities are heavily dependent on a community network of contacts that are more typical of suburban than urban lifestyles.

Lifestyles vary, of course, according to the type and quality of housing people can afford. Demand and supply may be roughly in balance in the aggregate, but affordable housing is inadequate for minorities or those with low incomes. Public policy will be struggling for some time to overcome the political and institutional obstacles to providing housing for all. In the face of uncertainty about national priorities, the only safe assumption forecasters can make is that dwelling units will be smaller, on average, because of the shrinking size of households and the rising cost of residential construction. A growing share of residential construction will be accounted for by multifamily dwelling units.

THE SOCIOPOLITICAL ATMOSPHERE

Countries are now so interconnected that U.S. isolationism, in either economics or politics, is highly improbable in the future. The technological revolution in information and communications is tearing down virtually all national economic barriers.

In some parts of the world, economic interdependence is eroding political boundaries and overcoming language barriers to create stronger and larger markets. The economic resurgence of Japan is well documented, and its advancing technological prowess is providing a new stimulus to peaceful competition with U.S. entrepreneurship and productivity. China appears to be emerging as a vast new market and an even vaster source of low-wage labor ready to be respected and feared as a competitor by all the industrial powers. The Soviet Union may be on the threshold of an economic restructuring that opens markets for consumer goods and encourages, in some sectors, direct foreign investment. And the United States, recovering from a productivity slump and a long spell of consumption at the expense of saving and business investment, is on the way to restoring its balance of trade.

The next decade could be one of expanding trade and restoration of the nation's comparative advantage in the production of basic commodities (especially from agriculture) and high-technology goods and services. Unemployment in this country may well remain at very low levels and underemployment may drop substantially. With proper education and emphasis on life-long training and retraining, many new entrants into the work force may enjoy the upward mobility hitherto beyond their reach.

With nations around the world seemingly in a mood to reduce confrontations and de-escalate conflicts, and with ideological competition and expansionism overshadowed by economic opportunities and greater consumer satisfaction, this country may be on the brink of an era when resources can be cautiously redirected from defense to the civilian economy. Thus, it may become possible to modernize aging urban infrastructures, to increase investment in health care and public education, to support more research and development in the public and private sectors, and ultimately strengthen incentives for private investment and programs to reduce poverty in America.

This scenario is not necessarily utopian but evolutionary. Progress is bound to be slow, interrupted or delayed by setbacks and the vagaries of the political process. But it is the direction that counts, and for those near the bottom of the economic ladder, the next decade may provide new opportunities, if only because a potentially tight job market will make people's labors more valuable and their wages more rewarding.

While world politics appear headed for calmer seas, at least in the nearer and more discernible future, a number of long-term developments—population explosions, disparities between rich and poor, energy shortages—bear watching for potentially de-stabilizing effects.

THE DEMOGRAPHIC SCHISM

The contrast between population growth rates in the industrialized countries and those in the developing world is dramatic, especially in the relative size of certain age groups, notably the young. In most of Latin America, for instance, young people under 15 years represent about 40 percent of the total population. In the United States and Canada, that proportion is just over 20 percent; in Western Europe and Japan, it is even lower. These imbalances mean that, over the next 20 years, Latin American countries will have to absorb proportionally twice as many entrants into their economies as the United States or Canada. Mexico alone has a population in excess of 80 million and is growing by more than 2 percent per year; at least 20 percent of it is unemployed (and underemployed). This situation is not atypical of other developing countries.

These population pressures are manifested in the rising number of illegal immigrants to the United States. The pool of potential entrants is large and growing. The Immigration Reform and Control Act of 1986, which provided amnesty for certain illegal aliens and penalties against employers hiring those not declared legal, was intended to deal with past, not future, problems. The practice of establishing labor-intensive manufacturing operations across the border to take advantage of this available labor pool is sure to grow, so long as wage differentials reflect the disparity in economic opportunity between the two countries.

The situation is potentially explosive and casts a pall on U.S.-Mexican relations. The issue of the illegal migrants remains on the national agenda, kept alive by the growing political awareness of Hispanic groups and the demand for labor by the expanding economy of the Southwest. Mexico's role as a potentially major supplier of natural gas to U.S. markets also cannot be disregarded.

The search for a better life is not limited to the Western Hemisphere. Immigration from the Pacific Rim will grow as the recent wave is successfully absorbed into the U.S. economic fabric. Following the long tradition of other immigrants, the Asian community will provide the magnet for dependents, refugees and other skilled immigrants. Pressures to pry open the gates to immigration may soon come from the Philippines, whose population of 60 million is expected to double in the next 25 years, whose birth rate is 25 percent higher than that of continental Asia and whose infant mortality is 40 percent lower. The consequence of such demographic trends is clear: some 750,000 people will seek to enter the work force every year. Thus, the spread of poverty in this country is symptomatic of the developing world's desperate need for an outlet. No other social force has greater potential for destabilizing the pace of global development, yet no massive relief measures currently are in sight.

OIL DEPLETION

Rising oil imports and the prospect of declining economic reserves in North America are cause for renewed concern over the nation's long-term energy security. The U.S. Navy's presence in the Persian Gulf is clear evidence of the industrial world's strategic dependence on the free flow of petroleum from the largest known reservoir of liquid fossil fuels. For at least the past 15 years, the linch-pin of this country's national energy policy has been the need to decrease dependence on imported oil. The OPEC actions of the 1970s, the recessions that followed and institutional adaptations to rapidly rising fuel costs have given the United States and other industrialized countries a respite from their growing dependence on the Middle East. But now, with the economic recovery of the 1980s, world demand is again rising; for the United States the growing volume of imported oil has become a principal cause of the nation's inability to cut down its unfavorable trade balance.

At present, there are no prospects for major oil field discoveries, and the search is becoming more costly and politically difficult. While oil continues to be a declining energy source for domestic generation of electricity, the prospect of price increases due to higher oil recovery costs and a strengthened cartel influences every facet of energy demand. For the consumer faced with decisions pivoting on considerations of energy efficiency, the prospect of higher Btu costs will become clearer as imports continue to rise, with or without the recurrence of discrete oil shocks. As always, forecasters are affected by the recent experience that has presented the world with oil prices far lower than anticipated just five years ago. Will the current oil supplies be absorbed and lead to real oil price increases? Will gasoline be taxed to reduce the nation's deficit? The future of oil is tangled in questions that cannot be answered today.

Current oil consumption trends probably will stir renewed political interest in energy policy that is less market driven. The oil-dependent transportation sector may be the first recipient of greater government involvement. The search for substitutes, including renewable resources and demand-side measures, probably will return to the top of the energy agenda in the 1990s and beyond. Oil will continue to play a commanding role in energy prices until the world's economy can reduce its dependence on depleting energy sources.

COPING WITH SOCIOPOLITICAL CHANGE

The sociopolitical arena lends itself to myriad scenarios with a full range of impacts upon the demand for energy. Almost any major action on the national or the international scene that changes the "normal" course of events will create effects that directly or indirectly alter the price of energy, the outlook for more or less regulation and consumer behavior. The very necessity of energy in the life of 5 billion people exposes it to the whims of political influences.

It is impossible to postulate a full gamut of developments that can influence the demand for energy. There simply are too many combinations of events and circumstances to array. Even so, energy planners must be able to gauge the principal implications of uncertainty.

FOR FURTHER READING

The following is a selected list of the sources consulted in developing this chapter's outlook. Each provides a more detailed treatment of the issues discussed in this chapter.

M.N. Baily and A.K. Chakrabarti, "Innovation and U.S. Competitiveness," *The Brookings Review,* Fall 1985, pp. 14-21.

B. Barker, et al, "The World of 2006," *EPRI Journal,* vol 12-2 March 1987, pp. 4-25.

Daniel Bell, "The World and the United States in 2013," *Deadalus,* vol 116-3, Summer 1987, pp. 1-31.

C. Fred Bergsten, "Economic Imbalances and World Politics," *Foreign Affairs,* Spring 1987, pp. 770-794.

M. Cetron, W. Rocha, R. Luckins, "Long Term Trends Affecting the United States," *The Futurist,* July-August 1988, pp. 29-40.

R.M. Cyert and D.C. Mowery (editors), *Technology and Employment: Innovation and Growth in the U.S. Economy,* National Academy of Science: Committee on Science, Engineering and Public Policy, National Academy Press, Washington D.C., 1987.

Data Resources Inc., "Structural Change in the United States: A Historical Analysis," Lexington, MA, September 1984. Report prepared for the Edison Electric Institute.

Peter F. Drucker, "The Coming of the New Organization," *Harvard Business Review,* January-February 1988, pp. 45-53.

Peter F. Drucker, "The Changed World Economy," *Foreign Affairs,* Spring 1986, pp. 768-791.

The Economist, "The World Economy: Living with Uncertainty," September 1987, pp. 55-56.

Electric Power Research Institute, "The Politics of Climate," vol 13-4, June 1988, pp. 4-15.

M. Godet and R. Barre, "Into the Next Decade: Major Trends and Uncertainties of the 1990s," *Futures,* vol 20-4, August 1988, pp. 410-423.

B.R. Guile and H. Brooks (editors), *Technology and Global Industry: Companies and Nations in the World Economy,* National Academy of Engineering, Washington, D.C., 1987.

G.N. Hatsopoulos, P.R. Krugman, L.H. Summers, "U.S. Competitiveness: Beyond the Trade Deficit," *Science,* July 15, 1988, pp. 299-307.

W.B. Johnson and A.H. Packer, *Workforce 2000: Work and Workers for the 21st Century,* the Hudson Institute, Indianapolis, Indiana, June 1987.

Frank Levy, *Dollars and Dreams: The Changing American Income Distribution,* Russell Sage/Basic Books, New York, 1987.

R. Landau, "U.S. Economic Growth," *Scientific American,* June 1988, pp. 44-52.

Jack R. Meredith, "The Strategic Advantages of the Factory of the Future," *California Management Review,* vol 29-3, Spring 1987, pp. 27-41.

Oxford Analytica, *America in Perspective: Major Trends in the United States through the 1990s,* Houghton Mifflin, Boston, 1986.

Peter G. Peterson, "The Morning After," *The Atlantic Monthly,* October 1987, pp. 43-69.

J.B. Quinn, J.J. Baruch, and P.C. Paquette, "Technology in Services," *Scientific American,* vol 257-6, December 1987, pp. 50-58.

U.S. President, *Economic Report of the President* "Annual Report of the Council of Economic Advisers," Chapters 1-3, February 1988.

U.S. Department of Commerce, "The Status of Emerging Technologies: An Economic/Technological Assessment to the Year 2000" Washington, D.C., June 1987.

U.S. Department of Commerce, Bureau of the Census, *Population Profile of the United States,* Special Studies Series P-23, No. 150, Washington, D.C., April 1987.

U.S. Department of Labor, Bureau of Labor Statistics, *Occupational Outlook Handbook,* 1988-89 Edition, Washington, D.C., April 1988.

U.S. Office of Technology Assessment, *Technology and the American Economic Transition: Choices for the Future,* Washington, D.C., May 1988.

Ralph Whitehead Jr., "New Collars, White Collars," *Psychology Today,* October 1988, pp. 44-49.

Daniel Yergin, "Energy Security in the 1990s," *Foreign Affairs,* Fall 1988, pp. 110-132.

John A. Young, "Technology and Competitiveness: A Key to the Economic Future of the United States," *Science,* July 15, 1988, pp. 313-316.

CHAPTER III.

Future Energy and Electricity Demand: The 1990s through 2015

The nation's energy future will be shaped by many influences over the next 25 years. They include the relative prices of available fuels, the composition of economic output and demands for resources, the nation's stock of buildings and appliances, the extent of incentives for energy efficiency improvements and the motivation and behavior of all consumers. Many outcomes for these variables are possible and many scenarios can be fashioned from combinations of possibilities.

For this report, the Project developed a Reference Case forecast that plays out a middle-of-the-road energy future. This is a case shaped primarily by what can be foreseen or logically assumed based on the direction of current developments—it encompasses no wild cards, no reaching for the unexpected or the improbable. This chapter focuses primarily on the results of the Reference Case forecast.

THE PROJECT'S REFERENCE CASE FORECAST

TOTAL ENERGY AND ELECTRICITY

The Project's forecast of U.S. electricity and end-use energy requirements—Figure 3.1 and Table 3.1—project end-use energy (including electricity) to grow at an average annual rate of .3 percent through 2000, then slow to 1.1 percent after 2000. Electricity requirements* are projected to grow, on average, at

---

*This includes both utility-delivered power and power generated on-site by customers for their own use.

TABLE 3.1
RESIDENTIAL
SECTOR

ENERGY AND
ELECTRICITY FOR
END USE

	1987	2000	2015
GROSS NATIONAL PRODUCT			
billion 1977$	2,505	3,462	4,75
avg ann growth rate, previous 15 years	2.7%	2.5%	2.1%
DELIVERED END USE ENERGY			
quadrillion BTU	54.8	64.8	76.
avg ann growth rate, previous 15 years	-0.3%	1.3%	1.
ELECTRICITY USE			
quadrillion BTU	9.1	12.6	15.
billion kilowatt hours	2,516	3,500	4,33
avg ann growth rate, previous 15 years	3.0%	2.6%	1.5%
share of total end use energy	16.5%	19.4%	20.4%

FIGURE 3.1
END USE
ENERGY—
U.S. TOTAL

NOTES: Totals include the requirements of the residential, commercial, industrial, and transportation sectors, plus the small "others" group. Electricity use includes both power purchased for end use an power generated by customers on-site for self use.

DELIVERED ENERGY, QUADRILLION BTU

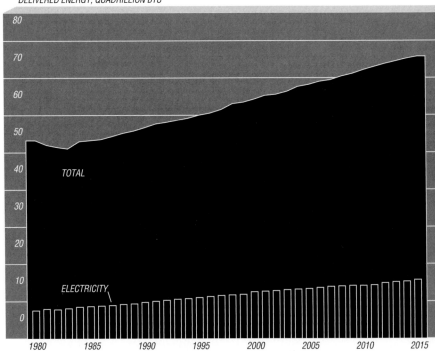

the rate of 2.6 percent through the year 2000—slightly ahead of the growth rate of real Gross National Product (GNP) and significantly ahead of total energy demand (Figure 3.2). In the 15 years after 2000, the demand for electricity also slows, with average annual growth at 1.5 percent—still ahead of total energy growth but lagging behind growth of real GNP.

Despite this slowing of growth in electricity requirements, the electrification of the economy increases throughout the forecast period. By 2015, electricity will account for more than 20 percent of the nation's total requirements for end-use energy, up significantly from less than 17 percent in 1987. Also, Table 3.2, which distinguishes future electricity requirements by consuming sector, indicates that industry's already dominant role in the mix of electricity demand will increase further, while commerce and residence requirements decline.

This forecast is the result of projections for the four major consuming sectors: residences, commerce, industry and transportation.* For completeness, the electricity forecast also includes a projection for the comparatively minor group of consumers listed as "others." Anticipated future developments—demographic trends, technology, energy prices, the shifting structure of the economy—and their implications for energy and electricity requirements are discussed later in this chapter.

The forecast bears out several major themes that form the prospects for the nation's energy future:

- As real economic growth slows and other factors remain equal, the demand for energy also slows. As a consequence, there will be greater competition among energy suppliers for customers.

- The country clearly has become more energy efficient since the OPEC embargoes. It has maintained economic growth—2.5 percent annually since the late 1970s—while experiencing an absolute decline in the energy consumed by households, commerce, industry and transportation over most of the period. Much energy waste has been eliminated and the most rapid payback investments in energy efficiency improvements already have produced results.

- Electricity will continue to increase its share of the total energy market. Despite OPEC-induced price shocks, demand for electricity sustained an average annual growth

---

*The forecast in this chapter is the outcome of an analytical effort drawing on several forecasting tools including the University of Maryland's INFORUM model of the U.S. economy, several sectoral end-use energy market models developed by the Electric Power Research Institute (REEPS for the residential sector; COMMEND for the commercial sector), and additional models developed for the Project by The Futures Group (industrial and transportation sectors). The Project's forecasting approach is described briefly in Appendix A.

TABLE 3.2
FORECAST TOTALS
SECTORAL MIX
OF ELECTRICITY
REQUIREMENTS

THE REFERENCE
CASE FORECAST

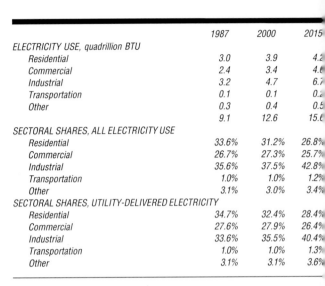

	1987	2000	2015
ELECTRICITY USE, quadrillion BTU			
Residential	3.0	3.9	4.2
Commercial	2.4	3.4	4.6
Industrial	3.2	4.7	6.7
Transportation	0.1	0.1	0.2
Other	0.3	0.4	0.5
	9.1	12.6	15.6
SECTORAL SHARES, ALL ELECTRICITY USE			
Residential	33.6%	31.2%	26.8%
Commercial	26.7%	27.3%	25.7%
Industrial	35.6%	37.5%	42.8%
Transportation	1.0%	1.0%	1.2%
Other	3.1%	3.0%	3.4%
SECTORAL SHARES, UTILITY-DELIVERED ELECTRICITY			
Residential	34.7%	32.4%	28.4%
Commercial	27.6%	27.9%	26.4%
Industrial	33.6%	35.5%	40.4%
Transportation	1.0%	1.0%	1.3%
Other	3.1%	3.1%	3.6%

FIGURE 3.2
COMPARATIVE
GROWTH
TRENDS

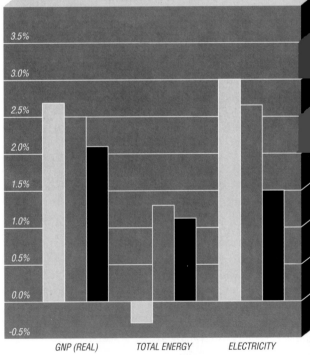

AVERAGE ANNUAL CHANGE %

GNP (REAL)   TOTAL ENERGY   ELECTRICITY

1972-1987   1987-2000   2000-2015

rate of 3 percent between 1972 and 1987, during a period of enhanced conservation and a computer/information revolution that created applications uniquely electricity dependent.

- For much of the next decade, the real price of electricity should remain stable. With its competitive strength and technology-driven applications in all sectors of the economy, electricity will have a marketplace of opportunity.

- Beyond year 2000, however, real electricity prices will rise as current generating facilities must be replaced and a new building cycle is funded. Investments in efficiency will be stepped up, life-cycle costing will become a pervasive decisionmaking criterion in all end-use markets and advanced technology developments may enhance the competitiveness of natural gas. In the post-2000 period, electricity will face a more slowly growing economy and more competitive energy markets.

ASSUMPTIONS ABOUT THE ECONOMY

The Project's projections of future electricity and energy requirements are based directly on a set of assumptions about the nation's long-range economic growth prospects and on a number of alternative pathways for the economy. From this process a mid-range case was selected. It is intended to be neither too optimistic nor too pessimistic, attuned to the forces for change discussed in Chapter 2 and representative of mainstream current thinking.

This scenario, presented in Figure 3.3 and Table 3.3, shows GNP (in constant 1977 dollars) increasing at an average annual rate of 2.5 percent through the year 2000, slower than the 2.7 percent average that characterized 1972 through 1987. After 2000, the rate of growth slows further to average 2.1 percent annually.

Growth in disposable personal income, also in constant dollars, follows a similar pattern, though modestly outpacing GNP growth. The GNP on a real per capita basis continues to grow at the same pace as the past 15 years. Of the major components of GNP, personal consumption accounts for essentially 59 percent of the total throughout the forecast period. Gross private domestic investment increases from less than 16 percent (1987) to nearly 17 percent by 2015. Exports expand from less than 9 percent currently to 13 percent by 2015. Government purchases decline from 17 percent to almost 11 percent by 2015. The present deficit in international trade (current account) moves to a surplus in 2000 and beyond.

FIGURE 3.3
THE FUTURE
U.S.
ECONOMY

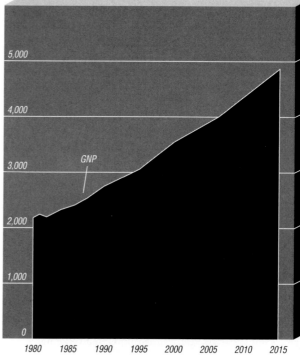

BILLIONS OF 1977 $

Source: A scenario developed by the INFORUM Group, University of Maryland.

MAIN ELEMENTS OF THE SCENARIO

- GNP grows (real) by 2.5 percent annually, through the year 2000; slower growth in the 15 years after 2000, by 2.0 percent annually;

- Production for export accounts for a sizably increasing share of GNP; the share of resources devoted to private domestic investment increases; the share of GNP for government purchases declines substantially; GNP per capita continues to increase in real terms, at a rate similar to that which characterized the last 15 years;

- Major influences behind the projections:
  - Slowing rates of population and labor force growth to 2000; slower rates in the 15 years after 2000;
  - Further integration of the U.S. domestic economy into the international economic system;
  - Widespread adoption of advanced technology, together with escalating international competition for goods and services;
  - Improving trends in productivity, but no return to the high rates of overall productivity growth that prevailed in the early 1960s.

The U.S. economy envisioned by this scenario is "upbeat" in important respects. It foresees quickening application of advanced technology, the retooling of plants and equipment for modernization and increased competitiveness, growing exports of goods and services and a substantial reduction of the federal budget deficit. On the other hand, the scenario's slower rates of overall economic expansion (i.e., real GNP growth) reflect improving but still modest productivity growth trends, changing demographics (particularly slower growth in population, house-

TABLE 3.3

KEY CHARACTERISTICS OF THE FUTURE ECONOMY

	1987		2000		2015	
OUTPUT AND INCOME						
Gross National Product						
billion 1977$	2,505		3,462		4,754	
avg ann growth rate, prev 15 years	2.7%		2.5%		2.1%	
components: billion 1977$, share of gross domestic product						
personal consumption	1,670	58.6%	2,236	57.2%	3,189	58.8%
gross private domestic investment	447	15.7%	650	16.6%	913	16.8%
exports of goods and services	248	8.7%	489	12.5%	707	13.0%
imports of goods and services	347	—	450	—	672	—
government purchases	486	17.0%	536	13.7%	617	11.4%
Personal Disposable Income						
billion 1977$	1,801		2,562		3,610	
avg ann growth rate, prev 15 years	2.7%		2.7%		2.3%	
Gross National Product per Capita						
1977$	10,297		12,885		16,327	
avg ann growth rate, prev 15 years	1.6%		1.7%		1.6%	
Personal Disposable Income per Household						
1977$	19,927		23,242		29,116	
avg ann growth rate, prev 15 years	0.6%		1.2%		1.5%	
DEMOGRAPHICS						
Resident population						
millions	243		269		291	
avg ann growth rate, prev 15 years	1.0%		0.8%		0.5%	
Households						
millions	90		110		124	
avg ann growth rate, prev 15 years	2.1%		1.5%		0.8%	
Civilian labor force						
millions	119		139		154	
avg ann growth rate, prev 15 years	2.1%		1.2%		0.7%	

Source: Economic Report of the President, 1988; Statistical Abstracts of the U.S., 1988; future scenario development by INFORUM.

hold formation and labor supply) and the intensification of global competition.

Changes in the composition of economic output also are significant for the scenario, especially for future electricity and energy requirements. The forecast postulates gradual continuation of the structural changes already under way. The production of tangible goods (in agriculture, mining, construction and manufacturing) maintains a very sizeable and stable share of overall output. But this stability masks significant changes in the parts that make up the whole. Shares in some segments of durables manufacturing (electrical and non-electrical equipment, computers, transportation equipment) increase while shares in agriculture, mining, construction and some segments of nondurables manufacturing (food products, textiles and printing) decrease. The service sector, which accounts for the lion's share of future employment growth, only gradually gains a share of total output over the forecast period, while transportation, communications/utilities, and services increase and wholesale and retail trade and the financial segments show declines.

THE RESIDENTIAL SECTOR

The electricity requirements of U.S. residences will increase from less than 3 quads currently to more than 4 quads by 2015. At the same time, consumer demand for all energy, including electricity, will grow very little—it will reach just 10 quads early in the 1990s and then remain there. As Figure 3.4 and Table 3.4 illustrate, this pattern reflects an average growth of electricity demand of 2.1 percent a year through 2000, then a substantial slowing from 2000 to 2015. For all energy, use grows 0.4 percent through the 1990s, then slows to virtually no growth in the 2000-2015 period. (By comparison, electricity's demand growth averaged 3.4 percent annually from 1972 through 1987 while total energy use actually declined over that period.) Overall, the forecast shows electricity accounting for an increasing share of the residential sector's total energy requirements, growing from more than 31 percent in 1987 to more than 40 percent in 2015.

The anticipated flattening of demand for both electricity and total energy is attributed to four factors:

- Demographic trends that will reduce the rate of household formation from 1.5 percent in 1985-2000 to only 0.8 percent in the subsequent 15-year period.
- Widespread use of energy-efficient appliances in existing homes as well as in new homes because of mandated appliance efficiency standards, rising energy costs and a shift toward marketing on a life-cycle cost basis.

DELIVERED ENERGY, QUADRILLION BTU

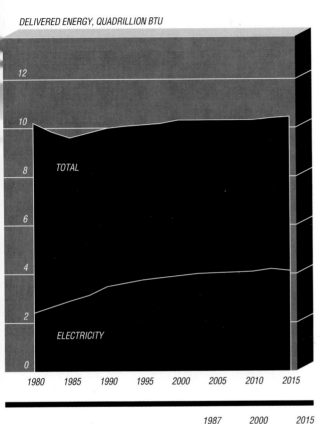

12

10

8   TOTAL

6

4

2

ELECTRICITY

0

1980   1985   1990   1995   2000   2005   2010   2015

FIGURE 3.4
**ENERGY USE
IN THE
RESIDENTIAL
SECTOR**

	1987	2000	2015
NUMBER OF HOUSEHOLDS			
millions	90.4	110.2	124.0
avg ann growth rate, prev 15 years	2.1%	1.6%	0.8%
DELIVERED ENERGY TO END USE			
quadrillion BTU	9.7	10.3	10.4
avg ann growth rate, prev 15 years	-0.4%	0.4%	0.0%
ELECTRICITY USE			
quadrillion BTU	3.0	3.9	4.2
avg ann growth rate, prev 15 years	3.4%	2.1%	0.4%
share of total end use energy	31.4%	38.0%	40.4%
ENERGY USE PER HOUSEHOLD			
million BTU per household	107.3	93.8	83.6
ELECTRICITY USE PER HOUSEHOLD			
million BTU per household	33.7	35.7	33.8

TABLE 3.4
**RESIDENTIAL
SECTOR**

**ENERGY AND
ELECTRICITY
FOR END USE**

- Substantial improvements in the thermal integrity of buildings, primarily new homes, but also older homes weatherized under the stimulus of utility incentives and the prospect of long-term energy cost increases.
- Significant competition from gas-fired heating and cooling equipment in the residential market, supported by end-use research and development in the gas industry and a potentially favorable outlook for the North American natural gas supply.

Just less than 60 percent of the residential sector's total energy requirements goes for space heating and cooling. Over the next 25 years, this requirement will grow more slowly than that for other energy uses in the home. This slow growth reflects in part the already high level of saturation of cooling equipment in many areas of the country. But buildings also will be tighter. Homes, on average, will become smaller, although there will be considerable variation in this trend across the nation's major socioeconomic groups. (Over time, many people will move to quarters with greater floorspace. But the demographics and economics of the next several decades promise continuation of the current emphasis on high density housing such as condominiums.) Also, improving efficiencies in heating and cooling equipment and greater attention to servicing will further contribute to a dampening of demand growth.

Smaller electrical appliances and illumination devices, on the other hand, will proliferate and the potential for home electronics is considerable. A growing range of electronic devices for home security, automatic energy management, communications, information and leisure activities are being developed. The rise of the "convenience factor," especially for two-worker families, will be a driving force in the spread of these technologies. Growing demand for leisure/recreation facilities in the home and using an increasing share of residential space for some kind of business/ professional service also will contribute to the momentum of the home electronics market. Many residential customers will be improving the quality and energy efficiency of their lighting equipment by replacing existing units with technology based on advanced fluorescent and long-life bulbs. The incentive programs of utilities in many parts of the country will play an important role in promoting this relamping.

MAJOR FORCES INFLUENCING RESIDENTIAL ENERGY DEMAND

Underlying this rise in residential energy demand are specific demographic, economic and technical forces. The demographic orces center on the slowing growth of both the general population and individual households. The rate of population growth slows as fertility remains low and the baby boom generation moves through its reproductive period. Household formation, which had been much more rapid than population growth in the 1960s and 1970s, also slows. It still remains nearly double the rate of population growth, reflecting, in part, the independent living preferences of young adults and the noninstitutionalized elderly throughout the 1990s. After 2000, though, the rates of household formation and population growth begin to converge, both falling to well below 1 percent a year. And as household formation slows, households get smaller because of lifestyle changes and the low birth rate.

The critical economic forces relate to household income and regional development. The forecast's projected rise in real household disposable income (by 1.2 percent annually to 2000, then by 1.5 percent in the 15 years after 2000) can be attributed to higher labor force participation rates and more productivity in all principal employment groups. Consequently, rising household income triggers more purchases and accelerated replacement of electricity-dependent equipment as well as higher use levels.

Over the long term, the West and South will account for a growing share of the U.S. population (as much as 80 percent of total population growth between 1980 and 2015), as both immigrants and internal migrants settle in these regions in response to economic opportunity and a living environment improved by the widespread application of climate controls.

These trends will increase customer usage for three reasons: household income relates directly to durable household expenditures; higher female employment creates demand for convenience equipment in the home; and the geographic shift of the population favors air-conditioning over space heating, the former being less subject to interfuel competition than the latter.

Technical forces influencing electricity demand are creating more efficient and more convenient homes. Research and development aimed at achieving more efficient energy uses is gaining market acceptance and will produce a new generation of appliances and equipment marketed on the basis of life-cycle cost considerations. At the same time, national appliance efficiency standards now in place will stimulate competitive marketing based on life-cycle cost advantages.

Housing construction practices are more energy-efficient than 20 years ago and resistance to removing obsolete building code features is lessening in many jurisdictions. Today, a typical new detached home uses about one-half the total energy needed for space conditioning in a comparable existing home. The thermal integrity of the housing stock (existing plus new) i expected to increase around 20 percent by 2015 because o improved construction practices, more wall and window insula tion and passive solar orientation. Centralized electronic control in new housing will do many things: enhance the efficiency o appliances; reduce wasted energy; promote thermal storage ir the home, and multiply the number of electric applications tha take advantage of electricity's versatility, controllability and loac management potential. The rapid spread of time meters anc differentiated rates will provide unparalleled opportunities fo more customer choices in the electronic home.

The average energy efficiency of space-heating equipment especially electric heat pumps, will improve, reducing suct energy requirements over existing housing stock by as much as 5(percent over the next 25 years. Heat pumps also will be used mor(as new housing starts rise in the South and West. Gas-driven heat pumps will not be competitive until late in the 1990s. Thei penetration initially will be impeded by a lack of gas distributior and equipment service networks in many areas of the South anc West. The load-management features of electric heat pumps under time-of-use pricing, however, should enhance electricity's competitive edge in this market.

WIDESPREAD EFFICIENCY MOVES RESIDENTIAL FORECASTS

Future growth rates of electricity use flatten particularly after 2000 mainly because of the combined effects of demographics and energy conservation in the home. The effects of slower household formation and smaller household sizes continue throughout the forecast period but become particularly influen- tial after 2000. The push toward improved energy efficiency also is strong, with total energy use per household decreasing 22 percent over the forecast period. Conservation is clear in the energy efficiency improvements in successive generations of residential appliances as well as in the materials and construction/ insulation practices adopted by builders and retrofitters to rein- force the thermal integrity of the housing stock.

The difference between the conservation measures taken immediately following the oil shocks of the 1970s and the efficiency-enhancement assumptions that underlie this forecast is that future reductions in energy use intensity will be perma- nent—they will be built into appliances, heating equipment and dwelling stock in both the replacement and the new housing markets.

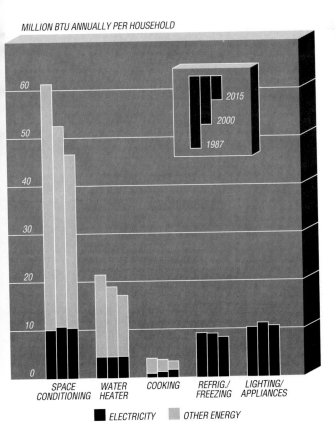

MILLION BTU ANNUALLY PER HOUSEHOLD

FIGURE 3.5
**RESIDENTIAL
ENERGY
INTENSITY
BY END USE**

A COMPOSITE
OF ALL
BUILDING TYPES

■ ELECTRICITY   ▨ OTHER ENERGY

END USE CATEGORY	1987	2000	2015
Space Conditioning	57.8%	56.2%	55.7%
Water Heating	20.9%	19.0%	19.1%
Cooking	4.1%	4.3%	4.1%
Refrigeration/Freezing	7.7%	8.8%	8.9%
Lighting & Other Appliances	9.5%	11.8%	12.3%
	100.0%	100.0%	100.0%

TABLE 3.5
**RESIDENTIAL
SECTOR**

**TREND IN
SHARES OF
END USE
CATEGORIES**

(AGGREGATE OF ALL
BUILDING TYPES)

EMERGING OPTIONS FOR SPACE CONDITIONING IN THE HOME

ADVANCED ELECTRIC HEAT PUMPS
Depending on the climate, the advanced heat pump with integrated water heating is expected to offer annual energy cost savings of 30-40 percent compared with the operation of the average heat pump now in use and separate electric resistance water heating. Performance analyses show the economic advantage of the advanced heat pump over other heat pump or gas furnace alternatives in a range of climates.

ANNUAL ENERGY COST (DOLLARS)

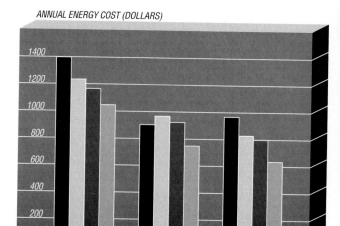

CHICAGO   ST. LOUIS   SAN ANTONIO

■ *INDUSTRIAL AVERAGE HEAT PUMP, RESISTANCE WATER HEATER*

□ *EFFICIENT GAS FURNACE, ELECTRIC AIR COND., GAS WATER HEATER*

■ *HIGH-EFFICIENCY GAS FURNACE, ELEC. AIR COND., GAS WATER HEAT*

▨ *ADVANCED HEAT PUMP (INTEGRATED WATER HEATING)*

OFF-PEAK HEAT STORAGE
Pennsylvania Power and Light Company has given about 3,500 owners of new houses bonuses of $1,000 to install heat-conservation systems which cost around $5,000 that use off-peak, night-time electricity to heat a special thermal storage reservoir in the house. During the daytime, when demand for the utility's power rises, these so-called "Four-Star Homes" use the heat in the reservoir to warm rooms and heat water. The company sells electricity to these customers for 3 to 4 cents a kWh instead of the usual daytime rate of 7 cents. The long-term payoff for all customers is in the load shifting effect off the system's daily peak and the potential for postponing the installation of additional peaking capacity.

Source: EPRI Journal, "The Advanced Heat Pump ... All the Comforts of Home," March 1988; New York Times, May 8, 1988, Section 10, p.18.

Future energy requirements by the average household and by major users are illustrated in Figure 3.5 and Table 3.5. The most dramatic change is the significant decline in average household energy requirements for space heating and cooling. This reflects several factors, including the improving thermal integrity of buildings, efficiency improvements in existing heating equipment, growing penetration of heat pumps and the gradual shift of the population to warmer climates where heat pumps are more competitive and where cooling requirements, while high, use fewer Btus than the heating needs of northerly households. But even with improving efficiency, space conditioning continues to dominate the residential energy use.

Average household requirements for water heating also show significant declines over the forecast period, largely the result of new equipment with improved efficiencies. Requirements for cooking show some marginal improvement based on improved technology as consumers replace older appliances. The same can be said for refrigeration and freezing.

On the other hand, lighting/appliances are a growth area, substantially enlarging their share of average household energy requirements. Important growth will come from expanding applications of electronic command-and-control over the living environment, vastly enhanced information and communication facilities (including devices for leisure/amusement), and a gamut of convenience appliances to serve multiple breadwinner households. All these will use technology already in place or in the process of commercialization and which is thoroughly electricity dependent at low intensity levels.

Countervailing forces, though, are also at work. More lighting units using advanced technology will lower electricity requirements for illumination. And automated household energy control systems are likely to cancel their own small direct increment to electricity use, yielding a net reduction in total household energy requirements through more efficient management. The balance of these technological advancements will only modestly add to energy requirements for lighting and appliances.

Total electricity consumption by the average household will remain much the same. It will rise somewhat in the 1990s as real electricity prices are stable or declining, and fall back after 2000 to essentially the 1987 level as efficiency enhancements become more widespread in response to price signals, public policy for efficiency standards and a variety of marketing incentives.

As shown in Figure 3.5, electricity will improve its share significantly in space conditioning and water heating uses. However, in the post-2000 period other technologies (e.g., natural gas heat pumps, solar systems with heat storage) may become competitive. Electricity for cooking will gain share throughout the forecast period due in part to the increasing use of such technology as microwave ovens. The refrigeration/freezing and lighting/appliances categories are completely electricity dependent.

THE COMMERCIAL SECTOR

The commercial sector will continue to account for a substantial share of the nation's total energy market even though growth rates will fall somewhat below the rate of commercial floorspace expansion. As indicated in Figure 3.6 and Table 3.6, the sector's total energy needs will grow from the current 6 quads to more than 8 quads in 2015. The rate of growth is likely to be higher in the 1990s, averaging 1.4 percent annually. After 2000, it slows to an average of just less than 1 percent annually.

For electricity, commercial sector requirements will grow substantially to 4 quads in 2015 from the current level of less than 2.5 quads. In the 1990s, electric use will grow by 2.7 percent annually and outpace the demand for all end-use energy as well as floorspace expansion. By 2000, electricity will account for almost 48 percent of total energy requirements of the commercial sector, a marked advance over the 1987 share of just more than 43 percent. Over the 2000-2015 period, electricity's growth slows to an average of 1 percent annually, paralleling both total energy use (0.9 percent) and floorspace expansion (1.1 percent).

The prospects for electricity in this sector will be influenced by several forces. There are substantial differences in energy requirements for various segments of commercial customers and the outlook for economic growth differs significantly from segment to segment. (The Project's aggregate forecast for the commercial sector is the sum of separate projections for the 11 segments identified in Table 3.7.) Also, growing pressures for improved productivity and competitiveness facing many U.S. service businesses in the years ahead will be met by advanced information technology (more computers, expanded telecommunications, artificial intelligence). These pressures will force a reconsideration of both manpower and building space requirements.

Economic pressures on both owners of commercial buildings and the businesses using space promise to escalate attention to the cost of energy and the need for efficiency enhancements involving building envelopes as well as technical improvements in appliances and equipment. Utility involvement in demand management is likely to encourage and accelerate this trend. And natural gas technology in absorption chillers and gas-fired heat pumps may compete successfully with electricity in some commercial markets. Lastly, the general slowdown in the overall expansion of the nation's economy, projected for the post-2000 period, will affect commercial energy requirements.

MAJOR FORCES INFLUENCING COMMERCIAL ENERGY DEMAND

ECONOMIC FORCES

The shift of the economy towards services-producing businesses provides an important basis for anticipating an expansion in the nation's commercial building stock and growing requirements for end-use energy and electricity. But this expansion will be tempered by mounting pressures from multinational organizations entering the U.S. market to provide services. Higher productivity through better technology, manpower reductions and ultimately lower floor space needs (per unit of output) will dominate decisions of U.S. commercial firms in the years ahead.

The commercial sector encompasses a variety of building types, each with a different mix of energy needs. Thus, to assess future energy demand, employment forecasts are needed for each of the principal components of the services industry:

- In wholesale and retail trade, employment is not expected to increase beyond its 1987-2015 share. But it will continue to constitute a very large segment (23-24 percent) of the entire services sector, with corresponding requirements for floorspace, including the replacement of obsolete or poorly located buildings.
- In "other services," which includes personal business and professional services, education and health, employment will increase its share from 23 percent in 1987 to almost 30 percent in 2015.
- In the **FIRE** (finance, insurance, real estate) category, employment will rise from 6.2 percent in 1987 to 7.8 percent in 2015. Clearly, the categories of **FIRE** and "other services" drive the demand for office space, which is expected to become more energy efficient under the stimulus of revised building codes, utility incentives and occupants' requirements for flexible layout and the accommodation of sophisticated office equipment. New office buildings will lead the way in a highly competitive market.

TECHNOLOGICAL FORCES

Productivity enhancements in the trade and services sectors will be increasingly technology driven. Technology already has

FIGURE 3.6
**ENERGY USE
IN THE
COMMERCIAL
SECTOR**

DELIVERED ENERGY, QUADRILLION BTU

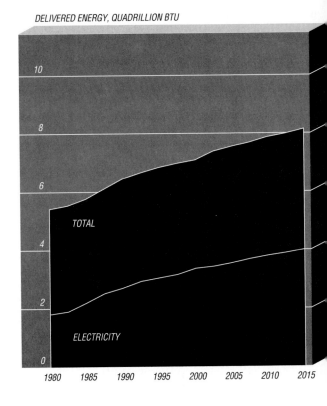

TABLE 3.6
**COMMERCIAL
SECTOR**

**ENERGY AND
ELECTRICITY
FOR END USE**

	1987	2000	201.
COMMERCIAL FLOORSPACE			
billions of square feet	55.9	71.8	85.
avg ann growth rate, prev 15 years	1.3%	1.9%	1.1%
DELIVERED ENERGY TO END USE			
quadrillion BTU	6.0	7.2	8.
avg ann growth rate, prev 15 years	0.6%	1.4%	0.9%
ELECTRICITY USE			
quadrillion BTU	2.4	3.4	4.
avg ann growth rate, prev 15 years	4.1%	2.7%	1.0%
share of total end use energy	40.0%	47.5%	48.7%
ENERGY USE INTENSITY			
thousand BTU per square foot	108.1	100.4	96.
ELECTRICITY USE INTENSITY			
thousand BTU per square foot	43.2	47.8	47

expanded the versatility of existing services and made totally new types of services practical (e.g., jet engine technology has vastly increased the demand for air transportation; human health care has been greatly expanded through diagnostic technology; and electronic information and communication technologies have stimulated innovations in distribution, engineering design, financial services, instant communications and the entertainment industry).

Large service companies now buy the latest technology (e.g., ATMs, package sorting and tracking technology, automated billing systems) and spread it across the world economy. For small service businesses, technology is providing the chief stimulus for "niche" entrepreneurship, that is, highly specialized service activities with a targeted market. A substantial share of employment growth in the services sector has come from creation and expansion of small firms that provide specialized support or analytical services for large corporations, enabling the latter to institute more effective cost controls and streamline their own operations.

In commercial building construction improved technology is being stimulated by three trends:

- More flexible code and materials requirements in a host of municipalities other than the older central cities. Most commercial growth is taking place in the suburbs.
- Rapidly growing requirements of office space users for climate control, computer and related electronic equipment, and flexibility in office layout to accommodate changing information/communication needs.
- Demonstration buildings backed by the research and development of diversified corporate organizations, introducing state-of-the-art systems aimed at lower maintenance and energy costs and testing results in a real-life setting.

ENERGY EFFICIENCY/LOAD MANAGEMENT

The outlook for rising energy prices (following a near-term hiatus in the 1990s) will revive the national drive toward higher end-use efficiency. Trends in relative energy costs affect the choice of fuel for structures typically built with a life expectancy of 50 years and more. Furthermore, decisions regarding energy efficiency measures are increasingly influenced by life-cycle cost considerations. Since the cost of energy represents a significant share of the annual operating and maintenance cost of commercial space, life-cycle cost computations are becoming a standard decision criterion for owners of commercial buildings.

Utilities are playing an increasingly important role in helping commercial customers improve energy efficiency that extends beyond conservation audits and information programs. A multitude of customer incentives are now in place. Assistance programs, such as those listed below, enable utilities to determine the level of subsidy required to achieve specific demand-management objectives:

- Loans or grants to large office builders for a design-team approach to energy-efficient construction.
- Rebates for thermal storage systems, automated thermostat and lighting controls.
- Lighting rebates for relamping commercial customers' premises with high-frequency ballast fluorescent light fixtures and for other features reducing daytime lighting requirements.
- Installation of low-emissivity windows.
- Utility-sponsored efficiency buy-back and shared-savings programs.

COMPETITIVE MARKET FORCES

The most potent force affecting the market for electricity is the pressure from growing use of natural gas. Gas may become increasingly competitive with utility-delivered electricity in a number of applications. For instance, packaged or standardized cogeneration systems will penetrate the commercial market particularly in office buildings, hotels, retail malls and large institutional buildings such as hospitals and colleges. Large requirements for hot water and steam, which depend on building type and use, will produce competition for cogeneration in the 10-1000 kw range. Gas heat pumps are expected to become competitive with electric heat pumps in the 1990s in certain commercial applications, but the degree of penetration will depend on prices as well as on gas supplies in hitherto underserved retail market areas. However, to compete successfully, the gas heat pump will require an efficient installation and service support, good operational control features and strong marketing. Space cooling with gas—cooling through a gas absorption chiller or through an electric chiller that uses electricity produced on-site in a gas-fed cogeneration unit—may become competitive as a result of the growth of cogeneration.

Gas will not be competitive, though, with electricity in the myriad services that depend on electricity-driven technology such as computers and other electronic and optical devices in the commercial sector. Nor is gas likely to become a serious threat in deep refrigeration.

COMMERCIAL FORECAST REFLECTS REFINED USES

Historically, the electricity requirements of commercial users have grown faster than those of other users. In recent years, the typical annual rate of growth has declined from the 7-10 percent range in the 1960s and the early 1970s to the approximately 4 percent between 1972 and 1987. (In a few recent years commercial sector growth has exceeded 4 or 5 percent in response to the sustained economic upturn and accelerated pace of commercial building activity.) Nevertheless, the growth rate will gradually slow over the next several decades.

Electricity may face increased competition in the post-2000 period because of rising real prices and the commercialization of technological advances based on other fuels (such as gas-fired heat pumps). But, on balance, electricity should maintain its overall competitive edge (as measured by saturation levels) in commercial energy markets in the years immediately ahead.

The marked slowdown in the post-2000 period in both total energy and electricity use reflects the confluence of several developments: cumulative investment in energy efficient office equipment, the increasing number of commercial structures with energy "smarts" and improved thermal integrity (both in new construction and through retrofits), some down-sizing of floorspace and manpower requirements (per unit of output) and the already-mentioned interfuel competition.

Understanding energy trends behind the aggregate forecast for this sector comes from examining a few of the end-use and segment-specific results (a more comprehensive report on these details appears in Appendix B). Figure 3.7 reviews the projected trends for the commercial sector as a whole and for major end-use requirements. In order to separate the effects of economic growth, the data in this figure are presented in terms of "energy intensity," that is, quadrillion Btu per square foot of floorspace. Figure 3.9 examines the projected trends in similar measures of energy intensity for each of the 11 commercial segments distinguished in the study. Here, data are presented for total end-use energy as well as for electricity alone. Figure 3.8 places these segment trends in perspective by summarizing the outlook for future expansion in each segment's stock of floor space.

These figures show the important trends in select segments of the commercial sector. All the commercial segments exhibit declining intensities for total energy use throughout the forecast period. Improvements in the thermal integrity of buildings and in the efficiencies of heating and cooling equipment account for much of this decline in nearly all of the segments (see Appendix B). Improvements in water heating also contribute.

Current electricity intensities are relatively high in most segments, with electricity's share of total energy ranging from 31 percent (health facilities) to 59 percent (groceries). These intensities will grow sharply in the 1990s when electricity enjoys price stability, and less so post-2000 as competition in energy markets increases. For all commercial segments, electricity's intensity and share of total end-use requirements will be significantly higher in 2015 than now because of increased penetration of electric technologies in space heating, cooling and cooking (see Appendix B). The growing use of advanced technology such as computers and communications equipment in many services-producing businesses, as reflected in the "miscellaneous" end-use category, also adds to the more intensive use of electricity.

Segments such as retail facilities and buildings in the "miscellaneous" category, which have comparatively low end-use energy and electricity intensities, will experience the greatest floorspace expansions over the forecast period. Hotels/motels and office buildings, with moderate energy intensities, will account for the next-largest floorspace expansions. High energy users, such as restaurants or groceries, will account for only a small share of the total commercial floorspace expansion.

For the commercial sector as a whole, the requirements for space heating and cooling will continue to dominate the end-use energy profile and show improving efficiencies. Lighting, with varied uses depending on segment, represents the second largest requirement by the commercial sector, though at a level well

ENERGY CONTROL SYSTEMS FOR "INTELLIGENT" COMMERCIAL BUILDINGS

Energy management and control systems help reduce energy waste through the automatic control of a building's energy using systems, including HVAC, lighting, and service hot water.

The basic components of a control system are the sensors, control actuators, field termination panels, modems, communication links, and the central control mechanism.

Such a system can be used in almost all new and existing commercial buildings to automate functions otherwise performed manually. Payback periods depend on the complexity of the installation and proper maintenance. Systems are available from over 200 manufacturers and range in cost from a few hundred dollars for single-function time clocks to multi-function systems ranging up to $1 million, depending on the number of points and microprocessors installed.

Every management system can be integrated with utility load control programs. It can provide a 10-20 percent energy use reduction in a commercial building providing it is suitably designed and reliably operated. In new office construction, electronic controls can be preplanned and designed to meet individual tenants' environmental, communications, and security requirements.

Source: Battelle-Columbus Division and Enviro-Management and Reserch Inc., DSM Technology Alternatives, EPRI Report EM-5457, 1987; A. H. Rosenfield and D. Hofemeister

below that required by space heating and cooling (see Appendix B). On balance, the need for better lighting becomes evident in the 1990s. But lighting efficiency improvements promised by advanced technology become a significant force after 2000. Energy requirements for water heating also are projected to decline significantly as equipment efficiencies improve. But this use accounts for only a modest share of the total. The "miscellaneous" category is a growth area because businesses of all types and sizes are expected to adopt information and communications technologies at an accelerating pace.

PROTOTYPE UTILITY-SPONSORED PROGRAM TO BUILD ENERGY EFFICIENCY INTO NEW COMMERCIAL CONSTRUCTION

PROGRAM PURPOSE:
 Utility-sponsored design assistance to stimulate architects, engineers, developers, and building owners into incorporating more energy efficient technologies into standard commercial building designs.

PROGRAM ELEMENTS:
- *Seminars and training for segments of the building community, including major real estate brokerage firms, regarding the benefits of energy efficiency in new buildings.*
- *Customized design assistance services to developers, architects, engineers, etc.*
- *Meetings of a "design team" to include architects, engineers, developers and building owners, as well as outside consultants where needed.*
- *Analytical assistance in calculating the impact of energy efficient technologies using a BIN or hourly computer simulation.*
- *Arranging for media recognition and publicity for participant buildings.*
- *Cast incentives for the procurement and installation of energy efficient technologies.*
- *Periodic reviews of program implementation goals and achievements.*
- *End-use metering of energy conserving measures in a sample of buildings.*

UTILITY INCENTIVES:
- *Defray costs of "design team" for work performed beyond standard building design to incorporate energy efficiency measures.*
- *Cash incentive to owner/developer to cover difference between the price of standard equipment and the energy-efficient upgrade. A cap is provided on the total utility contribution based on the utility's long-term avoided capacity cost calculations. Potential electric energy savings are calculated by computer simulation or by the architect/engineer for the building, with review by independent consultant.*
- *Once building is at least 75 percent occupied, utility will defray cost of an independent engineering consultant to conduct a post-occupancy audit to ensure that all measures are installed and are performing as designed. The consultant will make recommendations on operating and maintenance procedures.*

MARKETING APPROACH:
- *Through direct contacts with key decisionmakers (owner/developer), trade publication advertising, and distribution of an "energy-efficient design" guidebook to members of the building community.*

THOUSAND BTU ANNUALLY PER SQUARE FOOT

FIGURE 3.7
COMMERCIAL ENERGY INTENSITY BY END USE

A COMPOSITE
OF ALL
BUILDING TYPES

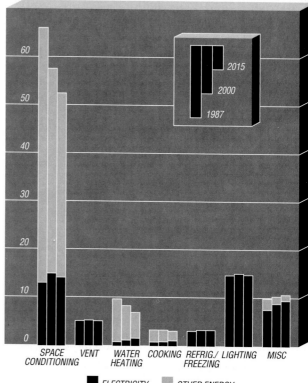

THOUSAND BTU ANNUALLY PER SQUARE FOOT

2015
2000
1987

SPACE CONDITIONING   VENT   WATER HEATING   COOKING   REFRIG./ FREEZING   LIGHTING   MISC

■ ELECTRICITY   ▨ OTHER ENERGY

TABLE 3.7
COMMERCIAL SECTOR SEGMENTS DISTINGUISHED

Restaurants
Health and Medical Facilities
Groceries
Hotels and Motels
Small-sized Office Buildings
Large-sized Office Buildings
Elementary and Secondary Schools
University and College Buildings
Retail Buildings
Warehouses
Other Miscellaneous Buildings

THE INDUSTRIAL SECTOR

Electricity will account for an increasing share of American industries, total energy requirements, rising from around 19 percent in 1987 to more than 23 percent in 2015. In actual quantities, industry's electricity requirements will increase from around 3 quads currently to almost 7 quads by 2015. Over that same period, this sector's demand for all end-use energy (including electricity) is forecast to grow from more than 17 quads to nearly 29 quads. This translates to an average growth rate in electric demand of 3.0 percent a year through the year 2000, then slowing to around 2.3 percent annually over the 2000-2015 period. Comparable rates for total end-use energy are 2.1 percent in the 1990s, slowing to 1.6 percent in the years 2000-2015

FIGURE 3.8
GROWTH IN COMMERCIAL FLOOR SPACE

FLOOR SPACE, BILLIONS OF SQUARE FEET

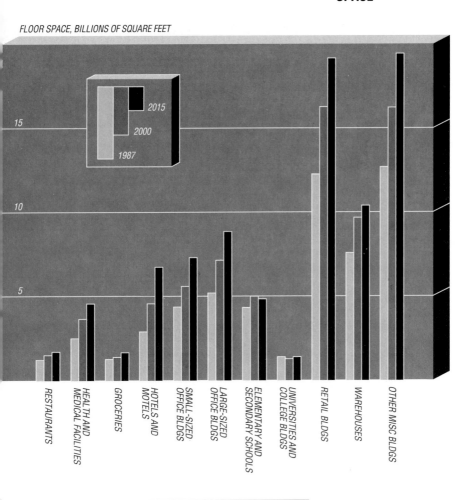

15

10

5

2015
2000
1987

RESTAURANTS

HEALTH AND MEDICAL FACILITIES

GROCERIES

HOTELS AND MOTELS

SMALL-SIZED OFFICE BLDGS

LARGE-SIZED OFFICE BLDGS

ELEMENTARY AND SECONDARY SCHOOLS

UNIVERSITIES AND COLLEGE BLDGS

RETAIL BLDGS

WAREHOUSES

OTHER MISC BLDGS

(Figure 3.10 and Table 3.8). (By comparison, electricity's demand growth averaged 1.9 percent annually from 1972 through 1987 while total end-use energy declined over the same period.)

Just two years ago, the nation echoed economists' concerns that heavy industry, much of it energy intensive, was suffering an irreversible decline in the United States. Indeed, the 1981-1982 recession, marked by a substantial drop in industrial output, caused the first absolute decrease in total electricity sales in more than 40 years, following several years of declining growth rates. But the experience of the late 1970s and early 1980s now has been reversed, and the demand for electricity by the industrial

FIGURE 3.9
ENERGY INTENSITY BY COMMERCIAL SEGMENT

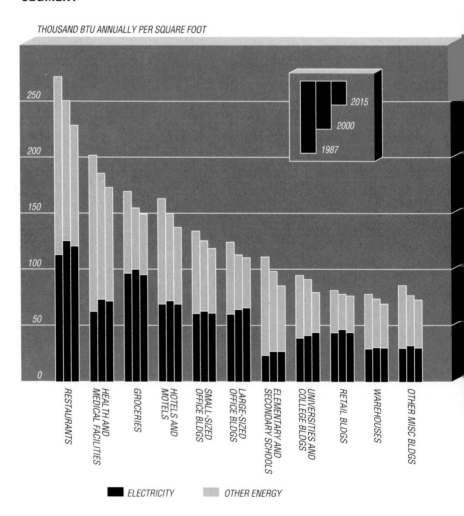

THOUSAND BTU ANNUALLY PER SQUARE FOOT

sector has been rising, tracking the resumption of growth in industrial output. This resurgence in manufacturing is due to sustained increases in productivity as well as the nation's regained competitiveness in response to the weaker dollar abroad.

Over the past decade, two forces have influenced industrial electricity use, including the substitution of electricity for fossil fuels. Namely, there are more opportunities for introducing electricity into a variety of manufacturing processes for greater operational efficiency, manpower substitution and quality control. Second, electricity offers increasing efficiency in existing applications, plants' operating environments and cost-cutting measures justified by rising energy costs.

These forces are roughly in balance at present. Industry has forged ahead of other major electricity users in institutionalizing conservation and modernizing assembly lines with greater energy efficiency as an explicit objective. Both forces promise to influence energy requirements in opposite directions for some time to come.

A third dimension of U.S. industry's electricity requirements is the structural change taking place within manufacturing. The intensity of energy and electricity requirements (i.e., quads per unit of economic output) varies among the many and diverse segments that make up the nation's manufacturing base. The past several decades have witnessed a significant expansion of the nation's less energy-intensive but high-value added industries (such as food products, non-electrical machinery, electrical equipment). Economists expect this structural trend to continue with these industry segments having the best prospects for maintaining a competitive edge in world markets. With the growing influence of lower energy-intense industries, the altered mix of manufacturing output has important implications for the future electricity requirements of the nation's total industrial sector.

MAJOR FORCES INFLUENCING INDUSTRIAL ENERGY DEMAND

Generalizations about the aggregate demand for electricity and end-use energy in the industrial sector reflect the enormous diversity of end uses. Industrial energy requirements can be usefully classified into major categories such as motor drive, electrolysis, process heat, lighting and other equipment. But, the mix of these categories varies extensively from one industry segment to another. The Project's industrial energy forecast is based on separate analysis of 23 industry segments, as identified in Table 3.9. And there is considerable energy-use diversity among the members of any one industry segment. Nevertheless, certain broad trends surrounding electrification, efficiency and electric uses common to all industry groups are apparent:

- The electrification of industry will continue as electricity is substituted for fossil fuels in such established activities as steelmaking (e.g., arc furnaces using scrap metal replaces open hearth technology using newly mined iron), process heating, chemical synthesis and fractionation, improved process control (so that electric intensity is much lower than that of competitive fuels), and advanced space conditioning and lighting investments.

- The production of such electricity-intensive products as primary aluminum, chlorine and certain petrochemicals will decline in the United States for competitive reasons, except to the extent that new processes (such as a yet-to-be commercialized smelting process) require less energy per unit of output.

- The electricity efficiency in all of its applications will continue to rise. For example, new electric arc furnaces will be better insulated and better control equipment will optimize the process. Electric motors, which account for about 65 percent of the total electricity used by manufacturing, are in the middle of efficiency improvements whose full impact cannot yet be assessed. Sales of energy-efficient induction and permanent magnet motors are growing rapidly. Electronic variable speed drives are penetrating the market for smaller motors, creating electricity savings averaging around 20 percent over traditional induction motors. Modern solid-state electronics and magnetic materials promise to revolutionize the design of motors and further broaden their application. As motor controls become less costly and more effective, they replace the traditional throttling by valves and baffles that have always been energy wasteful.

- The use of electricity in manufacturing will continue to reflect the increasingly complex operation of in-plant pollution control and waste management. In applications, equipment controls and motor drives are singularly electricity dependent.

In short, economic growth in the industrial sector will be supported by productivity-enhancing technology that is increasingly dependent on versatile electricity for controlling operations, for creating a better working environment and for advanced applications in process areas such as motors and heating. Improvements in the overall efficiency of energy use also will

DELIVERED ENERGY, QUADRILLION BTU

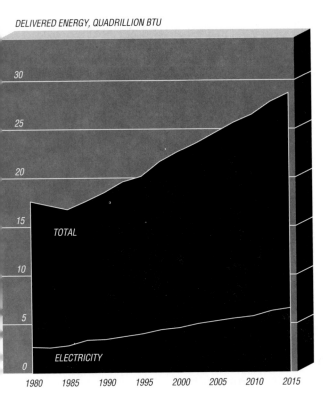

FIGURE 3.10
**ENERGY USE
IN THE
INDUSTRIAL
SECTOR**

	1987	2000	2015
TOTAL OUTPUT			
value of shipments, billions 1977$	2,018.3	2,974.6	4,215.8
avg ann growth, previous 15 years	2.7%	3.0%	2.4%
DELIVERED ENERGY TO END USE			
quadrillion BTU	17.4	22.7	28.9
avg ann growth, previous 15 years	-1.6%	2.1%	1.6%
ELECTRICITY USE			
quadrillion BTU	3.2	4.7	6.7
avg ann growth, previous 15 years	1.9%	3.0%	2.3%
share of total end use energy	18.5%	20.8%	23.1%
ENERGY USE INTENSITY			
thousand BTU per 1977$ of output	8.6	7.6	6.8
ELECTRICTY USE INTENSITY			
thousandBTU per 1977$ of output	1.60	1.59	1.59

TABLE 3.8
**INDUSTRIAL
SECTOR**

**ENERGY AND
ELECTRICITY
FOR END USE**

ADVANCED ELECTRO-TECHNOLOGIES FOR INDUSTRY

Process Industry Applications: chemicals, paper, food, petroleum/coal, textiles, tobacco.

Adjustable-speed drives. Semiconductor control circuits allow large electric motors to soft-start and vary speed to match loads, thereby conserving energy and reducing wear.

Freeze concentration. A refrigeration cycle is used to crystallize solvent, leaving a concentrated product. More efficient than evaporation and distillation methods, this technique is now used in food processing and could be applied in desalination and to a wide variety of aqueous solutions.

Heat pumps. Heat pumps absorb and compress heat for reuse. They are currently applied in food processing and electrolytic separation as well as in hot-water-driven absorption chillers. Heat pumps also have great potential for drying applications in the chemical, pulp and paper, and ceramic products industries and could be used for fractional distillation in the petroleum and chemical industries.

Electrolytic separation. This technology involves electrochemical processes in which reactants are maintained in an electrolyte and immersed electrodes apply voltage for separation. It is commonly used to produce chlorine and caustic soda.

Membrane processes. Membrane processes have a semi-permeable barrier—typically made of an organic polymer, metal or ceramic—to selectively transport components from one fluid to another. The driving force for the transport may be pressure, concentration, or electromagnetic gradient.

Metals Production Industry Applications: primary metals.

Direct arc melting. This is the most common electric melting method used today, accounting for a third of U.S. steel production. Once used mainly for high-alloy specialty steels, electric furnaces now produce a broad range of carbon and low-alloy steels.

Electrogalvanization. Electrolytic processes bond zinc or alloys to steel strip or plate for corrosion resistance. There is an expanding market for this technology in automobile bodies.

Electrolytic reduction. This technique uses electrical charge to separate pure metals from their compounds. In an electrolytic cell, a dc voltage is passed through an electrolyte containing metallic ions. Zinc, copper and manganese are produced using aqueous electrolytes.

Electroslag processing. An electrode formed from a metal to be processed is dipped into a chemical slag pool. When a dc current is run from this electrode through the slag pool to a base plate, the heat generated melts the tip of the metal electrode. The molten droplets thus formed fall through the slag pool where impurities are chemically removed.

Induction melting. Magnetic field-induced currents melt metal (or keep it molten) in foundry operations or for vacuum refining of high-alloy and specialty metals. The process is also used in holding furnaces for nonferrous metals.

Ladle refining. Ladle refining furnaces are similar to electric arc furnaces except that they have a higher depth to diameter ratio. These units allow the steel maker to reheat the steel to a precise temperature and refine the steel to extremely tight chemical specifications.

Plasma processing. Temperatures of 10,000 F or more can be maintained in plasma generated by high-intensity electric arcs. Rapid neat transfer and excellent controllability suggest that plasmas can be an efficient and economical medium for industrial materials processing, including direct reduction of iron ore, scrap remelting, surface hardening and recovery of metals from arc furnace dusts.

Vacuum melting. This technique encompasses a number of basic processes which are used to melt metal under a vacuum: induction melting, consumable electrode vacuum arc melting, electron beam melting. These methods are currently used for producing high-purity reactive and refractory metals, including many with aerospace applications.

Material Fabrication Industry Applications: non-electrical machinery, transportation, electrical equipment, fabricated metals, instruments, miscellaneous manufacturing, stone/clay/glass, rubber, lumber, printing, apparel, furniture, leather.

Electrical discharge machining. An electric arc produced by a high-voltage, pulsing dc source is used to erode the surface of a metal object to a desired shape. The technique is used extensively in die production (particularly for carbide tools) and to create small deep holes and narrow slots in metal parts.

Electrochemical machining. This technique is a metal machining process used by ferrous and nonferrous metals industries to produce complex shapes (high temperature alloy forgings, turbine wheels, jet engine blocks).

Electromagnetic and electrohydraulic forming. In EMF a bank of capacitors is used to generate a rapidly expanding magnetic field around a metal object to be formed; the force generated by the field drives the metal object against a die where it is formed. In EHF a rapid electrical discharge is generated across an electrode gap in a tightly sealed container of water or oil; the resulting shock wave in the liquid medium exerts intense pressure on a metal object, forming it against a die.

Electron beam heating and curing. In this technique a directed and focused beam of electrons is used to heat and cure materials (typically, metals and woods).

Electroplating. This is an electrochemical technique for depositing a layer of metal onto a surface in an electrolytic bath which contains a metal ion to be plated. The technique is widely used for finishing metal parts, chrome plating, metal foil production, wire and strip coatings, and the plating of electronics parts and jewelry.

Flexible manufacturing systems. Integrated machine tool assemblies make maximum use of computerization and automation to process a variety of finished parts without direct operator involvement; they afford increased productivity, improved quality control, and lower inventory requirements.

Induction heating. Heating of a metal from within is accomplished by placing a metal object inside a coil through which ac electricity flows. The resulting magnetic field induces eddy currents in a metal object, which in turn generate heat under subsequent dissipation. The technique is used for heating prior to metal work, heat treating, welding and metal melting.

Infrared drying and curing. The selective surface absorption of infrared energy by many industrial materials makes infrared technology ideal for drying and curing metals, wood products, textiles, and some electronic components.

Laser processing. Pulsed or continuous-power industrial lasers offer wide-ranging applications, including cutting, drilling, welding, surface treatment, and scribing of metallic, ceramic, and semi-conductor materials.

Microwave heating and drying. Microwaves between 300 and 300,000 MHz are used to heat and dry electrically nonconducting materials (dielectrics) composed of polar molecules. The greatest applications of microwave heating to date have been in industries that heat and dry moist materials (as water is a common polar molecule): the food industry, rubber products, and foundries.

Radio-frequency heating and drying. Like microwaves but at lower frequencies, electromagnetic radiation vibrates molecules of dielectric (nonconducting) materials to produce heat. Applications include drying of paper, preheating of plastics, and drying of glue in furniture and particle boards.

Resistance heating and melting. A material which is electrically resistant is heated or melted by passing an electric current directly through it or through an adjacent resistance heating element that transfers heat to it. An old and simple method of electrical heating, the technique is still widely used with some metals and in the glass industry.

Ultraviolet curing. Ultraviolet radiation is used to cure a variety of materials, i.e., to induce the rapid transformation of a liquid on a substrate to a solid coating. The process is used for coating applications, particularly to produce clear or slightly pigmented thin coatings.

ADVANCED ELECTRO-TECHNOLOGIES FOR INDUSTRY

Source: Resource Dynamics Corporation, Electrotechnology Reference Guide, EPRI Report EM-4527, R1, 1988; "Marketing Electrotechnology to Industry," EPRI Journal, April/May 1987.

continue, though probably with diminishing returns as older installations are phased out. (Enhancing the efficiency of energy use often serves as the justification for investment in new equipment. Or, it occurs as part of decisions aimed at gaining a competitive advantage over producers whose other costs may be lower.)

NEW APPLICATIONS BALANCE EFFICIENCY IN INDUSTRIAL FORECAST

The Project's forecast for the industrial sector shows a growth of electricity requirements at about the same rate as real industrial

---

ELECTRICITY USE AND THE FACTORY OF THE FUTURE

Over the next decade and beyond, pressures on U.S. industry to be globally competitive will stimulate the "remaking" of process activities across most SICs, with an eye to improved efficiency, cost leadership, and production flexibility. This future evolution of America's manufacturing is likely to include:

- The adoption of sophisticated design and management capabilities such as computer-aided design, computer-aided engineering analysis, and computer-aided planning and master scheduling
- Automation of production activities through computer-controlled manufacturing, flexible manufacturing systems, robots, and automated parts storage and retrieval
- Applications of advanced capabilities such as lasers and electrodischarges for machining and cutting, numerically controlled tools, plasmas and electron beams for heating and curing operations
- Other innovations, such as just-in-time scheduling and inventorying, "cellular" orientation, and efficient group classification and coding of components

Electricity is a critical component of many of these emerging systems—for refined process control, motorization, and energization—and it will be an energy form of increasing importance to U.S. industry in these applications.

The electricity intensity of the future factory will also be influenced by opportunities and strong cost incentives to improve the efficiency of most energy uses:

- The adoption of motors with better efficiencies and adjustable speed drives promises major electricity savings
- The effect of improvements in process design and automation for many industry sectors may be a net reduction of energy and electricity demand in many plants because of the greater control and task efficiencies provided
- Advanced technologies for electric process heating, electrolysis, machining and cutting, lighting, and space conditioning will create opportunities for efficiency enhancement
- Many electric utilities will be working with their industrial customers to hasten the adoption of energy efficient technology with the goal of retaining such customers on their system.
- The competition from other fuels will be strong. Progress is under way to develop advanced process technologies, especially those using natural gas.

Source: J. R. Meredith, "The Strategic Advantages of the Factory of the Future," _California Management Review,_ Spring 1987; A. Kahane and R. Squitieri, "Electricity Use in Manufacturing," _Annual Review of Energy,_ 1987.

Electric motors are the workhorses of the economy—in home refrigerators; in office heating and ventilation systems; in the many pumps, fans, compressors, and conveyors that power industrial processes. Approximately 60 percent of the electricity generated in the U.S. is used by electric motors; around 70 percent of the electricity consumed in the industrial sector goes for motor drive.

ADVANCES IN ELECTRIC MOTORS PROMISE LARGE ENERGY SAVINGS

Modern solid state electronics and new magnetic materials promise to revolutionize motor designs, providing considerably greater efficiencies and the potential for significant savings in unit electricity consumption.

In recent years, electric motor manufacturers have begun to produce lines of energy-efficient motors with significant improvements in efficiencies (see chart below). These improvements have been achieved through higher conductivity and larger cross-section conductors, increased core length, better magnetic materials, and reduced air gaps.

MOTOR EFFICIENCY

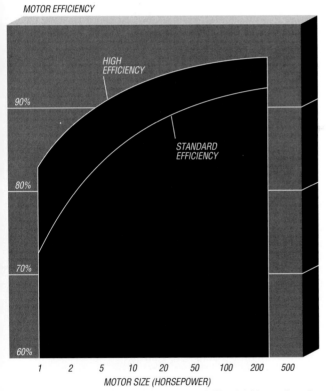

HIGH EFFICIENCY

90%

STANDARD EFFICIENCY

80%

70%

60%

1   2   5   10   20   50   100   200   500

MOTOR SIZE (HORSEPOWER)

FULL LOAD EFFICIENCY VERSUS SIZE FOR POST-1979 STANDARD AND ENERGY EFFICIENT 1800 RPM, 3 PHASE INDUCTION MOTORS

A second important development is the increasing availability of solid state electronic adjustable speed drives (ASDs) to closely match motor speed with the time pattern of load requirements. Research (including that by Lawrence Berkeley Laboratories) indicates that significant energy savings (10 percent or more for industrial applications) can be attained. Essentially, ASDs are power electronic systems that can provide a variable frequency output to AC motors; the ability to vary the frequency of power output provides a method of controlling the motor speed.

Source: S. Baldwin, "New Opportunities in Electric Motor Technology," IEEE Technology and Society Magazine, March 1986; Resource Dynamics Corporation, Electrotechnology Reference Guide, EPRI Report EM-4527, R1,1988; "Electronic ASDs Promise Huge Savings," Deed Digest (American Public Power Association), Spring 1988.

output (see Table 3.8). Total end-use energy requirements, on the other hand, will lag behind the growth of industrial output. Measuring energy as requirements per dollar (constant) of output, electric use is forecast to be about the same in 2015 as in 1978, while total end-use energy declines by more than 20 percent. In general, new applications of electricity generally compensate for the overall trend toward greater energy efficiency.

As noted, these aggregate trends emerge from complex combinations of developments that affect the many segments of

ENERGY FOR PROCESS HEATING IN MANUFACTURING— AN EMERGING MARKET FOR ELECTRICITY

For the manufacturing sector as a whole, energy needed for process heating represents the largest share of all energy used for heat and power, an estimated 83 percent in 1985. Heating plays an essential role in a wide spectrum of manufacturing processes: cooking, softening, melting, distilling, annealing, fusing.

Historically, firms have relied on fossil and by-product fuels to meet process energy needs; electricity currently accounts for only a very small share of process heat requirements, 2.6 percent in 1985. (There is great diversity across the manufacturing sector in the relative requirements for process heating—see Table 3.10 later in this chapter. But, electricity's overall role in meeting these needs is very low.)

New electrotechnologies with applications to process heating requirements, such as those listed below, are becoming commercially available and will provide future opportunities for electricity to compete in the process heat energy market:
Direct arc melting
Electron beam heating/curing
Electroslag processing
Induction heating/melting
Infrared drying/curing
Ladle refining
Microwave heating/drying
Plasma processing
Resistance heating/melting
Radio frequency heating/drying
Ultraviolet curing
Vacuum melting

The advantages of these technologies often go beyond their capability to substitute directly for existing process heat requirements. Many of the electrotechnologies provide radically new processing capabilities to manufacturing, such as electron beams and plasmas. Additionally, they are generally amenable to precise control and automation. Further, engineering studies indicate that they can contribute to opportunities for significant innovations in overall production systems.

Advanced electrotechnologies for process heating applications thus represent an important new market opportunity for electricity. On the other hand, competition will be strong, as fossil fuel technologies for process heat applications are also being improved.

Source: A. Kahane and R. Squitieri, "Electricity Use in Manufacturing" Annual Review of Energy, 1987; Resource Dynamics Corporation, Electrotechnology Reference Guide, EPRI Report EM-4527, R1, 1988; estimates by The Futures Group.

.S. industry in different ways. The forecast thus reflects the
1anging energy requirements of production facilities, the pene-
ation of end-use technology with improved energy efficiency
1aracteristics and the economic prospects for each industry
:gment. Figures 3.12 (A,B) and 3.13 (A,B) compare the
:onomic and energy use outlooks for each of the industry
:gments distinguished by the Project. (Additional details on the
:gment forecasts appear in Appendix B). Highlights of the
)recast, especially notable trends, are presented below:

1. The intensity of all energy requirements (measured as end-
use Btu required per constant dollar of output) will decline
throughout the forecast period and across all industry segments. Energy continues to be a sensitive component of
industry costs at a time when global competition is rising.
Industrial managers continue to look for ready targets in this
area and opportunities to reduce their costs. However, with
only a few exceptions, the intensity of electric use (Btu of
electricity required per constant dollar of output) remains
essentially stable.

2. The changing composition of industrial output signifi-

FFICIENCY BUY-BACK

CMP's Efficiency Buy-Back Program makes $2.5 million available to fund customer
ivestments in selected energy management projects. CMP will fund up to a
1aximum of half the project's installed cost, to reduce its simple payback period to
10t less than two years.

MP issued RFPs to its commercial and industrial customers in April and December
*f last year for potential energy saving projects. When proposals are received, they are
*ompared against each other according to the value of the energy to be saved, project
ost and reliability. CMP negotiates with customers whose projects rate highest
*gainst the above criteria.

*o be considered, projects must save at least 500,000 kilowatt-hours annually either
)y improving a system's efficiency or replacing electricity with a renewable or
*ndigenous to Maine fuel.

SHARED SAVINGS

Another program offered to commercial customers is Shared Savings. CMP provides
100 percent financing to accepted energy management projects up to a total of $5
million. Customers repay CMP from the actual savings on their electric bills for a
)eriod of up to five years. After that time, the customers realize all of the savings from
*he energy improvements. Three such projects are now under negotiation, including a
)roject to control the anti-condensate heaters on freezer doors in a chain of
supermarkets. This project would provide approximately 2.5 million kilowatt-hours of
*lectricity annually or about $125,000 per year savings to the customer. Overall,
CMP's goal is to obtain 10 million kilowatt-hours a year from this source beginning in
1988.

Source: Central Maine Power, Annual Report, 1987.

A UTILITY INITIATIVE TO STIMULATE ENERGY MANAGEMENT BY INDUSTRY

cantly influences total energy requirements as well as deman for electricity. The less electricity-intensive industrial se ments (See Table 3.9) account for both the highest grow rates and the highest levels of output. These industries als maintain their current electricity intensiveness over the for cast period. On the other hand, industries that are current highly-intensive energy and electricity users (Table 3. generally grow only modestly in output and decline in sha of total industrial output. These are mostly basic industri that continue to face competition from abroad and materi substitution (including recycled materials). With grow proportionately higher in industry sectors that tend to be le intensive energy users, overall economic growth will b accompanied by a lower growth in energy demand.

3. Two countervailing trends will influence electricity requir ments for industrial motors. First, future industrial process will require more motors per unit of output because of th

FIGURE 3.11
INDUSTRIAL ENERGY INTENSITY BY END USE

A COMPOSITE OF ALL INDUSTRIAL SEGMENTS

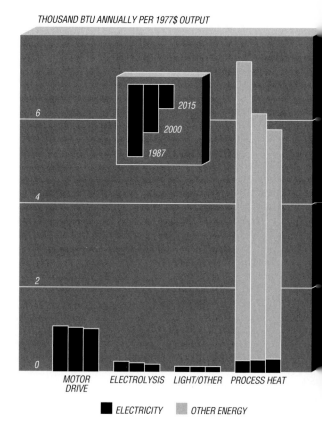

THOUSAND BTU ANNUALLY PER 1977$ OUTPUT

2015
2000
1987

6

4

2

0

MOTOR DRIVE   ELECTROLYSIS   LIGHT/OTHER   PROCESS HEAT

■ ELECTRICITY   ▨ OTHER ENERGY

needs of production processes and requirements for environmental controls. At the same time, electricity speed drive motors will penetrate increasingly into industry's stock of motors. The effect in most industries will be a net reduction in the electricity required for running motors per unit of output.

4. There will be widespread adoption of advanced information, automation and process control devices, computer-controlled flexible manufacturing systems, computer-aided design and robotics across the industrial sector in the next 25 years. These technologies are singularly electricity-dependent and represent important new markets for electricity in the industrial sector. However, they also represent comparatively low demand increments and may yield net reductions in overall energy and electricity intensities in many applications because of their efficiency.

5. Electricity plays a very small role in process heating while fossil fuels continue to dominate as illustrated in Figure 3.11. Advanced technology however, is creating opportunities for electricity in this area through microwave or plasma processing, electron beam heating, ultraviolet curing, electrobased chemical syntheses and separations. The use of these electric technologies will grow throughout the forecast period.

6. Self-generation by industry resumes a growth trend inter-

Agriculture
Mining and Resource Extraction
Construction
Manufacturing:
- SIC 20. Food and Kindred Products
- SIC 21. Tobacco Products
- SIC 22. Textile Mill Products
- SIC 23. Apparel and Textile Products
- SIC 24. Lumber and Wood Products
- SIC 25. Furniture and Fixtures
- SIC 26. Paper and Allied Products
- SIC 27. Printing and Publishing
- SIC 28. Chemical and Allied Products
- SIC 29. Petroleum and Coal Products
- SIC 30. Rubber and Miscellaneous Plastics
- SIC 31. Leather and Leather Products
- SIC 32. Stone, Clay, and Glass
- SIC 33. Primary Metals Industries
- SIC 34. Fabricated Metal Products
- SIC 35. Non-electrical Machinery
- SIC 36. Electrical Equipment
- SIC 37. Transportation Equipment
- SIC 38. Instruments and Related Products
- SIC 39. Miscellaneous Manufacturing

Table 3.9
INDUSTRIAL SECTOR SEGMENTS DISTINGUISHED IN THE STUDY

rupted in the 1960s and 1970s by low electric rates an rekindled by recent price declines as well as by opportuniti for cogeneration sales. No single industry segment is pr jected to meet most of its electricity requirements with sel generation by 2015, but growth will be significant in som groups, particularly those with large steam requirements an experience with self-generation.

THE TRANSPORTATION SECTOR

Transportation is a substantial and relentlessly growing user (energy—a sector in which the United States leads the rest of th world. The nation's unabating preference for personal transpo tation, its high per capita disposable income, the sprawling si of the country, its dense highway network and land-use patter that separate the workplace from the home, the shopping ar

FIGURE 3.12A
GROWTH IN INDUSTRIAL OUTPUT

ANNUAL OUTPUT, BILLIONS OF 1977 DOLLARS

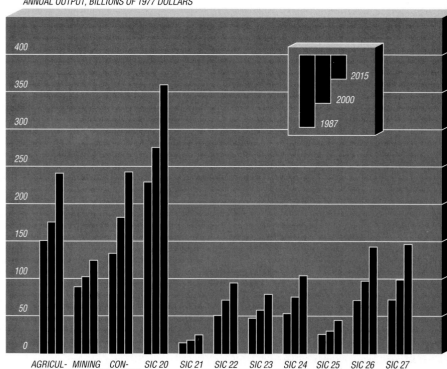

and leisure-time activities all contribute to this trend.

In 1987, the transportation sector accounted for the largest share of the nation's energy requirements—just more than 37 percent, with energy use by industry running a near second. Petroleum-based fuels provide nearly all of this sector's energy requirements. As Table 3.10 indicates, both natural gas and electricity contribute, albeit in minuscule shares compared with petroleum. Electricity, nevertheless, plays an important role in powering high-use passenger rail lines (including commuter, transit and intercity systems) and pipelines for the long-distance transportation of oil and natural gas.

In the future, the transportation sector's requirements for energy will increase from just more than 21 quads in 1987 to substantially more than 28 quads in 2015. As illustrated in Figure 3.14 and Table 3.11, this reflects an average rate of growth of 0.9 percent annually through 2000 and a slightly higher rate of 1.1 percent in the 15 years after 2000. (By comparison, this sector's total energy requirements grew on average by 1 percent annually

FIGURE 3.12B
GROWTH IN INDUSTRIAL OUTPUT

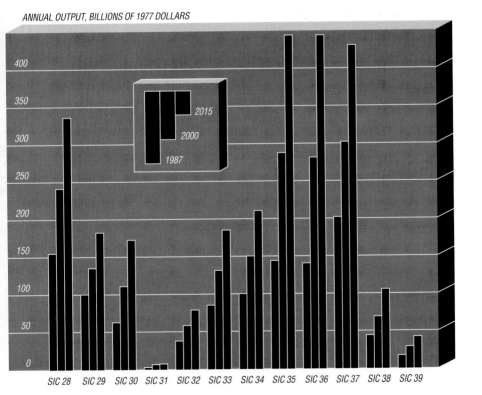

ANNUAL OUTPUT, BILLIONS OF 1977 DOLLARS

2015
2000
1987

SIC 28   SIC 29   SIC 30   SIC 31   SIC 32   SIC 33   SIC 34   SIC 35   SIC 36   SIC 37   SIC 38   SIC 39

over the 1972-1987 period.) The intrinsic demand for transportation services will be growing at faster rates, but the energy required (per unit) to supply these services will decline significantly, reflecting continued improvements in highway vehicle fuel use.

The transportation sector's requirements for electricity also should expand at a healthy pace. The Project forecasts requirements of just less than 0.2 quads in 2015, more than doubling the nearly 0.1 quads used in 1987. Some of this increase represents growth in current applications, for example, for railroads, public transit and pipelines. Some also reflects developments in advanced technology, particularly beyond the year 2000, as it begins to tip the scales in favor of electric vehicles for specialized usages. Even so, electricity will satisfy only a very small share of the nation's transportation energy needs because consumers appear to prefer the internal combustion engine.

FIGURE 3.13A
ENERGY INTENSITY BY INDUSTRIAL SEGMENT

THOUSAND BTU ANNUALLY PER 1977 DOLLAR OUTPUT

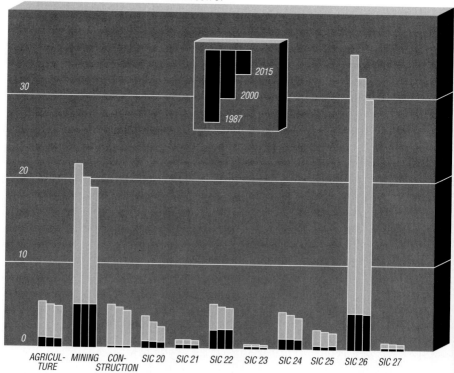

MAJOR FORCES INFLUENCING TRANSPORTATION ENERGY DEMAND

Demographic, economic and technical forces will influence the transportation sector just as they affect the other energy-using sectors of the economy. But electricity clearly plays only a minor role in providing for the U.S. population's mobility, and this will not be very different in the year 2015. The forces certain to increase the demand for personal transportation include:

- More people living in dispersed patterns as urban/suburban lifestyles merge in the sprawling metropolitan areas of the South and West and older central cities fail, in general, to stem the loss of workplaces.
- A larger labor force resulting in more commuter miles per household, typically leading to multiple car ownership.
- Rising disposable household incomes contributing to more vehicle ownership and more miles per vehicle.

FIGURE 3.13B
ENERGY INTENSITY BY INDUSTRIAL SEGMENT

THOUSAND BTU ANNUALLY PER 1977 DOLLAR OUTPUT

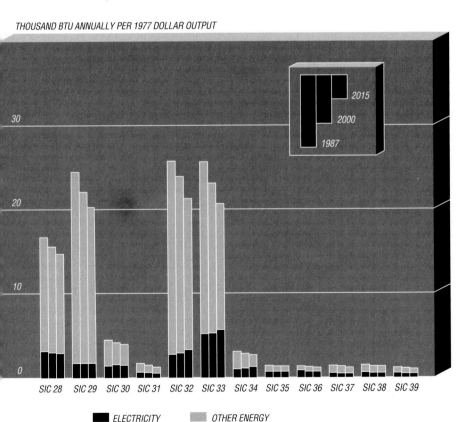

SIC 28 SIC 29 SIC 30 SIC 31 SIC 32 SIC 33 SIC 34 SIC 35 SIC 36 SIC 37 SIC 38 SIC 39

■ ELECTRICITY   OTHER ENERGY

TABLE 3.10
TRANSPORTATION SECTOR

HISTORICAL ENERGY AND ELECTRICITY CONSUMPTION

Selected Years: 1979, 1984
(quadrillion BTU)

	total	1979 petrol	nat gas	elec	total	1984 petrol	nat gas	elec
Highway	15.300	15.300			15.051	15.051		
Non-highway	4.481	3.787	0.612	0.081	3.988	3.364	0.540	0.085
air	1.539	1.539			1.633	1.633		
water	1.672	1.672			1.252	1.252		
pipeline	0.681		0.612	0.068	0.610		0.540	0.070
rail	0.583	0.576	0.000	0.013	0.495	0.480	0.000	0.015
freight	0.560	0.559		0.001	0.468	0.468		
passenger	0.029	0.017	0.000	0.012	0.026	0.011	0.000	0.015
transit	0.008			0.008	0.011			0.011
commuter	0.009	0.006		0.003	0.005	0.002		0.003
intercity	0.013	0.011		0.002	0.011	0.010		0.001
Military	0.648	0.648			0.679	0.679		
Total	20.429	19.735	0.612	0.081	19.718	19.094	0.540	0.085

Source: Oak Ridge National Laboratory, Transportation Energy Data Book April 1987 and preceding years

TABLE 3.11
TRANSPORTATION SECTOR ENERGY AND ELECTRICITY FOR END USE

	1987	2000	2015
DELIVERED ENERGY TO END USE			
quadrillion BTU	21.3	24.1	28.5
avg ann growth rate, prev 15 years	1.0%	0.9%	1.1%
ELECTRICITY USE			
quadrillion BTU	0.09	0.13	0.19
avg ann growth rate, prev 15 years	0.9%	2.6%	2.8%
share of sector total end use energy	0.4%	0.5%	0.7%

• Public transit not capturing a significant share of the commuter traffic despite major investment and operating subsidies in the larger urban centers. This is due to personal preferences for individual transportation and to the increasingly dispersed pattern of journeys to work along the periphery of metropolitan regions.

Technological forces (e.g., superconductivity applications in high-speed rail transport; improved storage batteries for electric cars) are likely to boost electricity but they will have to overcome powerful institutional barriers. For instance, the automobile industry is heavily committed to the internal combustion engine and the petroleum industry depends on a huge gasoline market. Also, travel on interstates, limited-access highways and longer commuter routes requires the versatility of cars. Reinforcing these attitudes is traditional public policy that tilts toward highway instead of mass transportation investment and the difficulties demonstrated by the U.S. experience with technologically advanced rapid transit systems. Lastly, governmental and community opposition to the acquisition and development

FIGURE 3.14
ENERGY USE IN TRANSPORTATION

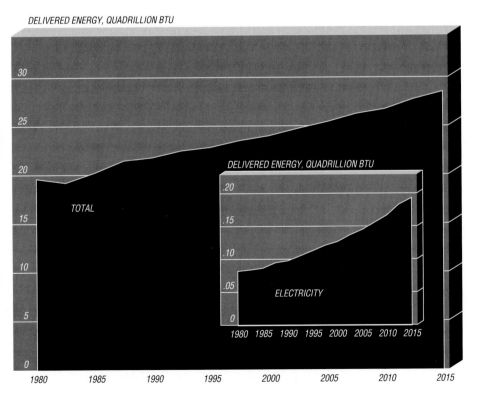

of new high-speed rights-of-way in densely settled areas favors non-electric personal transportation.

MARKET OPPORTUNITIES FOR ELECTRICITY

Market opportunities for electricity in the transportation sector, nevertheless, show promise for the next 25 years. They will arise in conventional applications as well as in new uses based on advanced technology. In public transportation, particularly conventional rail systems, expansion will occur parallel with economic and population growth, particularly within and between major metropolitan areas. Contributing to this expansion will be increasing congestion of intermetropolitan areas, thus favoring dedicated high-speed rail transportation. New developments in this area are likely to include increased conventional commuter train and rapid transit mileage from the larger central cities, new links between major airports and central cities and additional intercity railbeds, electrified for economic and air quality reasons.

Oil and gas recovery and transportation also offer new marketing outlets. Electricity requirements for pumping and compression will increase as deregulation of the natural gas industry leads to increased pipeline capacity for long-distance transportation and construction of additional links with Canada and perhaps Mexico. Another growing market is the expanding gas distribution grid in areas of the South and West, as well as in regions where gas can be used as fuel for electric utility and cogeneration facilities. Untapped gas resources from known and suspected reservoirs may be recovered and add to market demand.

Electric highway vehicles, in particular fleet vans driven for short distances and charged on rotation at central yards, will become more commonplace as advances in storage batteries and associated technologies finally yield improvements in cost and performance. Life-cycle economics for these vehicles will be a major concern to potential users, with road performance less important than low maintenance cost. Subcompact second or third cars for in-town or short commute transportation and easily charged at night will be used although initial cost and maintenance (including battery replacement) costs will be important competitive considerations.

Uncertainties in timing abound, however, because the electric car or van has yet to be commercialized, with no signs of any major corporation making the necessary investment in plant and service facilities. Competition from imported cars, together with federally imposed mileage efficiency targets, has kept Detroit

The average American (man, woman and child) currently travels about 13,500 miles per year. The average adult male spends just over 90 minutes daily in travel, spread evenly among trips for work, family, and leisure. While the amount of travel varies by type of household and by region of domicile, occupation, etc., distance and time have been increasing apace.

THE OUTLOOK FOR PERSONAL TRANSPORTATION IN THE U.S.

Numerous options could be available, especially for the journey to work. But the dominant theme this century has been the premium placed on individual mobility. In 1983, 86.4 percent of all automobile trips for business purposes and 65.7 percent of trips of all kinds were made by vehicles with single person occupancy (both up from 1977, when the shares were 81.2 percent and 59.6 percent respectively). Nothing is on the horizon to suggest any change in behavior—neither land use and housing decisions, the prospect of better public transportation, nor increases in vehicle operation costs. The future appears to belong to transportation systems that meet flexible personal service needs.

American dislike of public transit is longstanding (except in the largest cities with vital central business districts such as New York and San Francisco). Between 1970 and 1980, real family income declined, the number of workers living in urban areas increased by 15 million, large new public transit systems were built, government subsidies allowed transit prices to rise by only 44 percent, while the cost of owning and operating an automobile increased by 250 percent. Yet ridership on public transportation fell from 9 percent of all journeys to work to 6 percent, and the use of personal vehicles for the same trip increased from 80 to 86 percent.

Transportation's share of U.S. petroleum use keeps growing, making ever more serious (in economic and social terms) the spectre of future disruptions in the supply and cost of international oil. On the other hand, the technology of the internal combustion engine is advancing rapidly. Prototype developments in Sweden and Japan are yielding diesel-driven cars which can achieve fuel efficiencies of 71 miles per gallon, are light weight (50 percent the weight of the average U.S. car), meet air pollution standards, have better acceleration, and can be mass-produced at the cost of present subcompacts. The impending adoption by car manufacturers of continuously variable transmissions and flywheel energy storage is expected to boost overall efficiency to 90 miles per gallon.

Source: U.S. Office of Technology Assessment, Technology and the American Transition, 1988; M.C. Holcomb et al., Transportation Energy Data Book, Oak Ridge National Laboratory, Edition 9, 1987; D. Blevis, The New Oil Crisis and Fuel Economy Technologies: Preparing the Light Transportation Industry for the 1990s, 1988.

from taking risks with a new technology and developing a new market. Renewed federal emphasis on even higher fuel efficiencies with lower emissions probably will dominate industry planning in the 1990s. However, with more stringent air quality standards in the 1990s, particularly for the more congested metropolitan areas and the long-term cost advantage for electricity (particularly at off-peak rates) over petroleum products, the scales may begin to tip in favor of the electric vehicle, initially in such specialized applications as delivery vans dispatched by centrally serviced commercial facilities.

Advanced, high-speed rail transportation systems probably will be built. Advances in electric drive systems (through developments in superconductivity, magnetic levitation and related technical areas) will provide the technology for high-speed bullet trains or other special railbed transportation. This is primarily a post-2000 opportunity, however, with demonstration facilities from Europe and Japan possibly entering commercial use within 10 years.

TRANSPORTATION FORECAST SHOWS STEADY ELECTRICITY GAINS

The Project's forecast for this sector reflects a continuing growth in the nation's demand for transportation services although energy use will be constrained by public and national security policy as well as economic incentives to achieve significant gains in fuel performance. This is not an unreasonable assumption given the U.S. automobile industry's near doubling in fuel economy since the mid-1970s. The ratio of overall energy requirements for transportation per dollar of real GNP will decline 30 percent over the forecast period, from 8,500 Btu in 1987 to less than 6,000 in 2015. The rate of progress in this improvement slows after the year 2000 as opportunities for new gains diminish.

The major sources of the transportation sector's projected requirements for electricity are summarized in Figure 3.15 and Table 3.12. Most of the need throughout the 1990s stems from the requirements of pipelines and rail systems. This reflects essentially current applications and conventional technology expanding in step with the nation's economy. Beyond the year

THE COMMER-CIALIZATION OF ELECTRIC VANS

The electric van of the 1990s will incorporate two technological improvements—a high performance battery and an AC power train. These will give electric vehicles the range and speed to compete in a number of commercial markets.

Use of the lithium-sulfide battery, now ready for testing in a vehicle, results in a better range per charge, better acceleration, and higher top speeds than provided by current lead-acid batteries.

The power train, slated for 1990s van, will use an AC induction motor that will be about 50 percent lighter and 75 percent less expensive than an AC motor of comparable power. Transistors in small, lightweight power inverters will change the battery's DC power into AC power for the motor. Advantage: 10 percent lower initial vehicle cost at a constant range per charge, or a 10 percent greater range at a constant lifecycle cost.

Development and testing of these improvements are currently supported by EPRI.

Source: EPRI Journal, January/February 1988.

?000, however, new applications have a more substantial impact >n transportation's requirements for electricity. By 2015, elec- ric-powered vehicles—primarily commercial vans and short- distance autos for household use—will account for 10 percent of ransportation electricity. Also by 2015, though not visible on he chart, a small share of the rail system electricity will serve everal high-speed train lines.

The forecasted impacts of electric technologies in the trans- portation sector reflect the mid-range economic conditions of he Project's scenario. More robust economic conditions could accelerate penetration and result in more overall electricity demand. But the rate at which these technologies are commer- cialized is subject to many forces, including resistance to change by a vast, increasingly multinational industrial complex. The high cost (first cost, life-cycle operation and maintenance costs) of electric vehicles relative to existing personal transportation per- sists as a barrier to penetration, with few indications of a public policy to institute major changes.

ALTERNATIVE DEVELOPMENTS THAT COULD MAKE A DIFFERENCE

The Project's scenario is not a blueprint for the future. As recent history has shown, uncertainty is more prevalent than

HIGH-SPEED TRAINS

Germany is ready to market the world's first high-speed magnetic levitation train, capable of traveling above a steel track at speeds in excess of 300 miles per hour. The current U.S. target is a high-speed link between Los Angeles and Las Vegas for which a contract may be awarded by the Nevada-California Bi-State Commission in 1989. If completed in the mid-1990s, at an estimated cost of $2.5 billion, the project could carry 4-5 million passengers a year, taking considerable pressure off overcrowded airspace and rendering unnecessary additional highway construction between the two cities.

It is expected that France's T.G.V. high-speed train, now in commercial operation between Paris and several regional centers, will also enter the competition, but its speed is closer to that of the Japanese bullet train (200+ miles/per hour) than of the speedier German Transrapid.

The Transrapid, now operating on a test track in North Germany, is propelled by magnets attached to the track. It cannot be derailed since the body wraps around the rail. It requires less right-of-way than a conventional rail track, can negotiate steeper gradients, and avoids obstacles. It is, therefore, cheaper to build this track than that of a conventional railroad.

The success of this competitive bid may well set the stage for more inter-city high- speed links in the post-2000 years.

Source: New York Times, July 1, 1988 (p.D1).

certainty in the energy markets.

The forecast here has been built from a number of reasonable assumptions about the behavior of energy users in the face of changing technology, lifestyles, energy prices and a dynamic global economy. But future events cannot be fully anticipated and will be altered by developments whose timing and impacts are likely to affect the demand for energy. Also, many changes in the future will be the result of deliberate choices in response to new challenges faced by consumers, business and government. Alternative scenarios can be designed to represent situations where end-user demand will differ from this forecast in many ways.

Future developments that could sufficiently affect energy markets enough to warrant alternative scenarios include:

- Major breakthroughs in energy technology and utilization efficiency, particularly in such applications as transportation and manufacturing.
- Political events causing sharp or sustained changes in the cost and availability of petroleum, and all energy prices.
- Important legislative/regulatory developments in the environmental or the economic arena that might affect both the structure of energy delivery systems and the price of energy.
- Rates of national economic growth that, for any number of reasons, would depart from the mainstream assumptions in the Project's current economic growth outlook.
- Demographic trends reflecting either a much higher or lower rate of population growth than now expected or a geographic redistribution of the nation's population that differs from the "go West and South" pattern established in recent decades.

Further, any forecast scenario that creates significant changes in future electricity requirements has the potential of causing significant feedback effects on the price of electricity, the availa-

TABLE 3.12

TRANSPORTATION SECTOR

MAJOR COMPONENTS OF ELECTRICITY USE

	1987	2000	2015
TOTAL ELECTRICITY USE			
quadrillion BTU	0.090	0.126	0.191
MAJOR COMPONENTS			
Rail			
quadrillion BTU	0.016	0.022	0.030
share of total	17.6%	17.5%	15.8%
Pipelines			
quadrillion BTU	0.074	0.103	0.141
share of total	82.4%	81.4%	73.8%
Electric-powered vehicles			
quadrillion BTU	0.000	0.001	0.020
share of total	0.0%	1.1%	10.4%

ility and cost of capital needed to sustain growth and to replace
ging supply capacity, and the regulatory environment. Such
effects could, in turn, have legislative or regulatory conse-
quences, with impacts on demand-side decisions affecting all
kinds of end uses.

DELIVERED ENERGY, QUADRILLION BTU

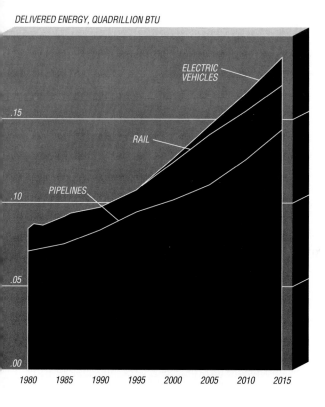

FIGURE 3.15
**MAJOR
ELECTRICITY
USES IN
TRANSPORTATION**

APPENDIX A

Overview
of the Project's
Forecasting
Approach

The forecast presented in this report is the result of an analytical effort by the Project staff utilizing several separate computer models to simulate U.S. economic growth and associated requirements for electricity and all energy sources.

The Project's forecast of total electricity and end-use energy requirements over the 1988-2015 period has been built up from individual consideration of future developments in each of the major consuming sectors: residences, commercial establishments, industry, and transportation. The projection for each sector directly reflects the Project's outlooks for the economy (economic growth, income, etc.) and relevant energy market conditions (fuel prices, competing fuels and technologies, prospects for self-generation, etc.).

ECONOMIC PROJECTIONS

The economic conditions assumed by the Reference Case for 1988-2015 are based on a comprehensive simulation of the U.S. economy prepared for the Project by the INFORUM group at the University of Maryland. INFORUM's econometric model contains an extensive input/output specification of U.S. industrial and commercial sectors, as well as details on U.S. trade with foreign nations.

INFORUM prepared several simulations during the course of the Project, utilizing alternative assumptions about future trends in key areas such as demographics, productivity, international trade, and government[1], Edison Electric Institute and The Futures Group, with the consultation of INFORUM, selected a case from this set to serve as the basis for the Project's energy forecasts.

As discussed in Chapter 3, the economic outlook chosen for the Reference Case reflects current mainstream expectations regarding the prospects for long range U.S. economic growth. It adopts, in brief, the Bureau of the Census current "middle series" demographic projections and assumes continuation of the improved overall productivity picture of the last six years, a significant movement during the 1990s toward balancing the federal budget and international trade accounts, and further gradual structural shifts in the composition of the economy.

ENERGY AND ELECTRICITY PROJECTIONS

RESIDENTIAL SECTOR. The Residential End-Use Energy Planning System (REEPS) software, developed by the Electric Power Research Institute, served as the methodological base for the residential energy projections [2.]

REEPS is an econometric/engineering model which simu lates the end-use behavior and fuel choices of the spectrum c residential energy consumers. REEPS accounts separately fc energy requirements in eight end-use categories: space heating air conditioning, water heating, cooking, dishwashing, refrigera tion, freezing, and miscellaneous. Different types of residentia buildings (existing dwellings and new construction) and th socioeconomic status of the households residing in them are als distinguished. For each of the household types and end us categories, REEPS forecasts appliance purchases (by fuel type appliance efficiencies, and rates of appliance utilization. A tot forecast for the sector results from an integration of all thes elements. Basic inputs to the model include information on fu prices, appliance options and costs, socioeconomic characteri tics of households, dwelling characteristics, and climate.

In order to meet the needs of the Electricity Futures Projec the software was operated in its "national" mode (which recog nizes differences among the major regions but yields only aggre gate results for the U.S. as a whole). Initially, Battelle prepare a REEPS simulation, utilizing exogenous assumptions from th Reference Case economic outlook (primarily, household socic economic characteristics) and the Project's expectations fc future fuel prices in the residential energy market[3]. To complet the forecasting process for this sector, The Futures Grou amended the REEPS results in order to incorporate the lates available statistics on energy use (through 1987) and to accoun (through, principally, application of TFG's Trend Impac Assessment process[4]) for long range changes in technology an energy market conditions consistent with the Reference Cas outlook.

COMMERCIAL SECTOR. The Commercial End-Us Energy Planning System (COMMEND) software, also deve oped by the Electric Power Research Institute, served as th methodological base for the commercial energy projections [5.]

COMMEND is an econometric/engineering model whic simulates the end-use behavior and fuel choices of major types c commercial energy consumers. Eleven commercial segments a distinguished in the model, based on generic type of building an nature of economic activity: restaurants, health facilities, groce ies, hotels & motels, small office buildings, large office building colleges & universities, elementary & secondary education, war houses, and miscellaneous. COMMEND accounts for the er ergy requirements of each segment in eight end use categorie space heating, ventilation, cooling, refrigeration, water heating cooking, lighting, and other (all with appropriate distinctions fc xisting buildings and new construction). For each commercial egment and end use category, COMMEND forecasts appli- nce/equipment purchases (by fuel type), end use efficiencies, nd rates of appliance/equipment utilization. A total forecast for he sector results from an integration of all these elements. Basic nputs to the model include information on building character- stics and floorspace requirements, technology options and costs, nd fuel prices.

In order to meet the needs of the Electricity Futures Project, he software was operated in its "national" mode (which recog- izes differences among the major regions but yields only aggre- ;ate results for the U.S. as a whole). Initially, Battelle prepared COMMEND simulation, utilizing exogenous assumptions rom the Reference Case economic outlook (estimates of future loorspace requirements by commercial segment) and the Pro- ct's expectations for future fuel prices in the commercial energy narket[6]. To complete the Project's forecast for this sector, The utures Group modified the COMMEND results to incorporate he latest available energy use statistics (through 1987) and to ccount (through TFG's Trend Impact Assessment process) for ong-range changes in technology and energy market conditions onsistent with the Reference Case outlook.

INDUSTRIAL SECTOR. A comprehensive spreadsheet imulation model was developed for the Project by The Futures ;roup to forecast future industrial requirements for energy.

The model distinguishes 23 industry segments: agriculture, nining, construction, and the manufacturing classifications SIC !0 through 39. For each such segment, energy requirements are ccounted in four major end use categories: motor drive, electro- ytics, process heat, and lighting/other. The dynamic portion of he model utilizes "unitized" expressions of each segment's nergy requirements by end use category (i.e., Btu per real dollar f economic output)[7]. The forecasting process involves project- ng the future trend in each unitized energy requirement cate- ;ory and then singling out electricity's share, consistent with the utlook on technology change and energy market conditions. A otal forecast for the industrial sector is prepared by scaling the nitized segment projections according to the future level of conomic output projected for each segment.

The Project's forecast for this sector is a national aggregation f segment detail[8]. The projections reflect the Project's segment- y-segment assessment of the impacts of numerous future devel- pments. In addition to the changing composition of economic utput, these include such items as the penetration of motors vith improved efficiencies, the adoption of controls for process utomation, pollution control requirements, the penetration of advanced technologies in uses such as process heating, and trends in self-generation of electricity.

TRANSPORTATION SECTOR. Forecasts of transportation sector energy requirements were developed by The Futures Group, based on the Trend Impact Assessment process[9].

Projections of future energy requirements (for both fossil fuels and electricity) from conventional transportation applications (i.e., airplanes, motor vehicles, railways, pipelines, military) were prepared to reflect the pace of economic expansion assumed in the Reference Case, and improving energy efficiencies in transportation technology. Prospects for penetration of new electricity-using technologies in this sector over the timeframe of the forecast — electric-powered vehicles (several types) and advanced rail systems — were assessed and integrated probabilistically with the projected requirements from conventional applications.

REFERENCES

1. Margaret McCarthy, "INFORUM Forecasts for the EEI Project," January 7, 1988 and October 5, 1988. Department of Economics, Interindustry Forecasting Project, University of Maryland.

2. The Electric Power Research Institute: *Residential End-Use Energy Planning System,* July 1982 (EPRI EA-2512); *REEPS Code: User's Guide,* January 1987 (EPRI EM-4882-CCM).

3. A. Faruqui and P. Hummel, "REEPS Simulations for the EEI Project," April 1988, Battelle.

4. The Futures Group, "Trend Impact Analysis," 1983, (TFG Working Paper). Trend Impact Analysis (TIA) is a general purpose modelling software developed by TFG to project and examine the influences of probabilistic future events on trends in system variables. TIA has been used widely in scenario development and other forecasting applications, where uncertain and/or novel future developments contain the potential to "deflect" or fundamentally alter the course of current trends.

5. Electric Power Research Institute: *An Implementation Guide for the EPRI Commercial Sector End-Use Energy Forecasting Model: COMMEND*, Volume 1: Model Structure and Data Development, June 1985 (EPRI EA-4049); *The COMMEND Planning System: National and Regional Data Analysis,* March 1986 (EPRI EM-4486).

6. A. Faruqui and P. Hummel, "COMMEND Simulations for the EEI Project," April 1988, Battelle.

7. The database for the industrial model was developed with reference to sources including: Bureau of the Census, *Annual Survey of Manufactures,* 1979-1985; Energy Information Administration, *Manufacturing Energy Consumption Survey,* 1985; Resource Dynamics Corporation, *Electrotechnology Reference Guide,* April 1986 (Electric Power Research Institute Report EM-4527).

8. M. Boroush and P. Stern, "Industrial Sector Energy End-Use Forecasts for the EEI Project," August and October 1988, The Futures Group.

9. M. Boroush and P. Stern, "Transportation Sector Energy Forecasts for the EEI Project," May 1988, The Futures Group.

APPENDIX B

Further Forecast Results

- RESIDENTIAL SECTOR
- COMMERCIAL SECTOR
- INDUSTRIAL SECTOR
- TRANSPORTATION SECTOR

	1987	2000	2015
NUMBER OF HOUSEHOLDS			
millions	90.4	110.2	124.0
avg ann growth rate, prev 15 years	2.1%	1.6%	0.8%
DELIVERED ENERGY TO END USE			
quadrillion BTU	9.7	10.3	10.4
avg ann growth rate, prev 15 years	-0.4%	0.4%	0.0%
ELECTRICITY USE			
quadrillion BTU	3.0	3.9	4.2
avg ann growth rate, prev 15 years	3.4%	2.1%	0.4%
share of total end use energy	31.4%	38.0%	40.4%
ENERGY USE PER HOUSEHOLD			
million BTU per household	107.3	93.8	83.6
ELECTRICITY USE PER HOUSEHOLD			
million BTU per household	33.7	35.7	33.8

ELECTRICITY'S ROLE IN MEETING END USE NEEDS
(aggregate of all building types)

	1987	2000	2015
Space Conditioning			
all energy, mill BTU per household	62.0	52.7	46.6
electricity, mil BTU per household	9.9	10.9	10.3
electricity's share	16.0%	20.7%	22.1%
Water Heating			
all energy, mill BTU per household	22.4	17.8	15.9
electricity, mil BTU per household	4.1	4.1	4.3
electricity's share	18.3%	23.1%	26.7%
Cooking			
all energy, mill BTU per household	4.4	4.0	3.4
electricity, mil BTU per household	1.2	1.3	1.5
electricity's share	27.5%	33.1%	43.4%
Refrigeration & Freezing			
all energy, mill BTU per household	8.2	8.2	7.5
electricity, mil BTU per household	8.2	8.2	7.5
electricity's share	100.0%	100.0%	100.0%
Lighting and Other Appliances			
all energy, mill BTU per household	10.2	11.1	10.3
electricity, mil BTU per household	10.2	11.1	10.3
electricity's share	100.0%	100.0%	100.0%

RESIDENTIAL SECTOR ENERGY AND ELECTRICITY FOR END USE

THE REFERENCE CASE FORECAST

ENERGY AND ELECTRICITY USE IN THE COMMERCIAL SECTOR

	1987		2000		2015	
TOTAL, ALL SEGMENTS						
floor space, millions sq ft	55,980		71,860		85,027	
avg ann growth, previous 15 years	—		1.9%			1.1%
END USE ENERGY INTENSITIES	thousand BTU per square foot annually, percent in form of electricity					
total	108.07	40.0%	100.43	47.6%	96.56	48.9%
space conditioning	65.16	20.5%	56.15	26.7%	53.34	26.1%
ventilation	4.46	100.0%	4.60	100.0%	4.47	100.0%
water heating	8.66	15.7%	7.91	20.9%	7.04	25.3%
cooking	3.10	26.8%	3.02	33.6%	2.84	39.2%
refrigeration	3.13	100.0%	3.34	100.0%	3.17	100.0%
lighting	14.45	100.0%	14.79	100.0%	14.46	100.0%
miscellaneous	9.11	61.9%	10.62	69.4%	11.24	73.7%
END USE ENERGY NEEDS, quadrillion BTU						
total requirements	6.05		7.23		8.24	
fossil/renewables	3.63		3.84		4.35	
electricity	2.42		3.44		4.01	
avg ann growth, previous 15 years						
total end use energy	—		1.4%		0.9%	
electricity (purchased + self gen)	—		2.7%		1.0%	
RESTAURANTS						
floor space, millions sq ft	1,200		1,565		1,833	
avg ann growth, previous 15 years	—		2.1%			1.1%
END USE ENERGY INTENSITIES	thousand BTU per square foot annually, percent in form of electricity					
total	269.87	43.1%	249.60	49.8%	230.52	51.5%
space conditioning	84.40	33.6%	75.14	40.0%	72.01	35.9%
ventilation	8.20	100.0%	8.52	100.0%	7.98	100.0%
water heating	54.84	15.0%	47.05	19.4%	39.75	22.9%
cooking	66.51	23.5%	60.47	30.2%	54.36	35.6%
refrigeration	23.86	100.0%	24.95	100.0%	23.93	100.0%
lighting	22.37	100.0%	23.13	100.0%	22.22	100.0%
miscellaneous	9.69	100.0%	10.35	100.0%	10.26	100.0%
END USE ENERGY NEEDS, quadrillion BTU						
otal requirements	0.32		0.39		0.42	
ossil/renewables	0.18		0.20		0.20	
electricity	0.14		0.19		0.22	
avg ann growth, previous 15 years						
total end use energy	—		1.5%		0.5%	
electricity (purchased + self gen)	—		2.6%		0.7%	

ENERGY AND ELECTRICITY USE IN THE COMMERCIAL SECTOR

	1987		2000		2015	
HEALTH FACILITIES						
floor space, millions sq ft	2,500		3,285		,244	
avg ann growth, previous 15 years	—			2.1%		1.7%
END USE ENERGY INTENSITIES	thousand BTU per square foot annually, percent in form of electricity					
total	200.60	31.2%	182.49	39.4%	167.71	43.1%
space conditioning	130.68	16.7%	110.78	22.4%	99.04	24.3%
ventilation	7.87	100.0%	8.24	100.0%	7.87	100.0%
water heating	18.97	15.1%	16.31	22.6%	13.72	27.8%
cooking	2.75	26.0%	2.75	41.3%	2.55	46.8%
refrigeration	0.36	100.0%	0.57	100.0%	0.48	100.0%
lighting	20.04	100.0%	20.73	100.0%	20.04	100.0%
miscellaneous	19.93	44.9%	23.11	55.3%	24.01	61.6%
END USE ENERGY NEEDS, quadrillion BTU						
total requirements	0.50		0.60		0.72	
fossil/renewables	0.34		0.37		0.43	
electricity	0.16		0.24		0.30	
avg ann growth, previous 15 years						
total end use energy	—		1.4%		1.2%	
electricity (purchased + self gen)	—		3.2%		1.8%	
GROCERIES						
floor space, millions sq ft	1,200		1,550		1,786	
avg ann growth, previous 15 years	—			2.0%		0.9%
END USE ENERGY INTENSITIES	thousand BTU per square foot annually, percent in form of electricity					
total	165.17	57.8%	155.69	64.1%	148.88	63.8%
space conditioning	77.90	18.2%	66.71	23.7%	63.22	22.3%
ventilation	5.96	100.0%	6.09	100.0%	5.70	100.0%
water heating	4.21	17.7%	4.13	29.4%	3.93	29.0%
cooking	3.29	22.7%	2.68	22.7%	3.08	37.0%
refrigeration	45.48	100.0%	46.86	100.0%	44.45	100.0%
lighting	24.60	100.0%	24.95	100.0%	23.93	100.0%
miscellaneous	3.73	100.0%	4.26	100.0%	4.56	100.0%
END USE ENERGY NEEDS, quadrillion BTU						
total requirements	0.20		0.24		0.27	
fossil/renewables	0.08		0.09		0.10	
electricity	0.11		0.15		0.17	
avg ann growth, previous 15 years						
total end use energy	—		1.5%		0.6%	
electricity (purchased + self gen)	—		2.3%		0.6%	

ENERGY AND ELECTRICITY USE IN THE COMMERCIAL SECTOR

	1987		2000		2015	
HOTELS AND MOTELS						
floor space, millions sq ft	2,880		4,526		6,441	
avg ann growth, previous 15 years	—		3.5%		2.4%	
END USE ENERGY INTENSITIES	thousand BTU per square foot annually, percent in form of electricity					
total	162.57	39.4%	148.36	46.7%	138.86	47.2%
space conditioning	77.47	31.3%	65.66	39.0%	63.57	34.9%
ventilation	4.97	100.0%	5.25	100.0%	4.88	100.0%
water heating	30.97	14.0%	27.07	19.4%	22.59	23.1%
cooking	12.95	26.4%	12.56	33.4%	11.26	38.8%
refrigeration	1.24	100.0%	1.26	100.0%	1.18	100.0%
lighting	17.09	100.0%	17.22	100.0%	16.65	100.0%
miscellaneous	17.88	48.6%	19.34	54.3%	18.75	59.2%
END USE ENERGY NEEDS, quadrillion BTU						
total requirements	0.47		0.67		0.90	
fossil/renewables	0.28		0.36		0.49	
electricity	0.18		0.31		0.42	
avg ann growth, previous 15 years						
total end use energy	—		2.8%		1.9%	
electricity (purchased + self gen)	—		4.2%		2.0%	
OFFICES, SMALL						
floor space, millions sq ft	4,280		5,718		7,130	
avg ann growth, previous 15 years	—		2.3%		1.5%	
END USE ENERGY INTENSITIES	thousand BTU per square foot annually, percent in form of electricity					
total	135.50	42.4%	125.40	50.2%	119.52	49.6%
space conditioning	93.54	24.1%	81.23	29.8%	74.90	26.1%
ventilation	4.39	100.0%	4.46	100.0%	4.29	100.0%
water heating	6.87	18.2%	5.64	26.4%	5.27	29.9%
cooking	0.89	46.8%	0.87	56.9%	0.75	56.9%
refrigeration	0.63	100.0%	0.66	100.0%	0.72	100.0%
lighting	19.65	100.0%	19.84	100.0%	19.18	100.0%
miscellaneous	9.52	90.0%	12.68	92.6%	14.41	94.4%
END USE ENERGY NEEDS, quadrillion BTU						
total requirements	0.58		0.72		0.85	
fossil/renewables	0.33		0.36		0.43	
electricity	0.25		0.36		0.42	
avg ann growth, previous 15 years						
total end use energy	—		1.6%		1.2%	
electricity (purchased + self gen)	—		3.0%		1.1%	

ENERGY AND ELECTRICITY USE IN THE COMMERCIAL SECTOR

	1987		2000		2015	
OFFICES, LARGE						
floor space, millions sq ft	5,230		6,997		8,719	
avg ann growth, previous 15 years	—			2.3%		1.5%
END USE ENERGY INTENSITIES	*thousand BTU per square foot annually, percent in form of electricity*					
total	120.71	49.6%	112.47	56.9%	109.94	59.4%
space conditioning	73.77	27.1%	62.15	32.3%	58.84	33.3%
ventilation	7.18	100.0%	7.16	100.0%	6.90	100.0%
water heating	7.09	19.3%	6.66	22.3%	5.82	28.1%
cooking	0.90	56.9%	0.85	63.8%	0.73	63.8%
refrigeration	0.68	100.0%	0.68	100.0%	0.70	100.0%
lighting	18.99	100.0%	19.19	100.0%	18.71	100.0%
miscellaneous	12.09	92.0%	15.79	94.2%	18.24	94.9%
END USE ENERGY NEEDS, quadrillion BTU						
total requirements	0.63		0.79		0.97	
fossil/renewables	0.32		0.36		0.43	
electricity	0.31		0.44		0.57	
avg ann growth, previous 15 years						
total end use energy	—		1.7%		1.4%	
electricity (purchased + self gen)	—		2.8%		1.6%	
ELEMENTARY AND SECONDARY SCHOOLS						
floor space, millions sq ft	4,330		4,865		4,760	
avg ann growth, previous 15 years	—		0.9%		-0.1%	
END USE ENERGY INTENSITIES	*thousand BTU per square foot annually, percent in form of electricity*					
total	110.60	19.2%	96.16	25.9%	86.59	28.9%
space conditioning	74.88	6.9%	61.52	11.6%	54.64	13.3%
ventilation	1.45	100.0%	1.50	100.0%	1.58	100.0%
water heating	15.00	6.9%	13.06	10.0%	11.12	12.4%
cooking	2.97	20.9%	2.88	26.0%	2.58	30.5%
refrigeration	0.41	100.0%	0.37	100.0%	0.39	100.0%
lighting	10.74	100.0%	11.04	100.0%	10.64	100.0%
miscellaneous	5.15	36.1%	5.79	48.5%	5.64	52.4%
END USE ENERGY NEEDS, quadrillion BTU						
total requirements	0.48		0.47		0.41	
fossil/renewables	0.39		0.35		0.29	
electricity	0.09		0.12		0.12	
avg ann growth, previous 15 years						
total end use energy	—		-0.2%		-0.8%	
electricity (purchased + self gen)	—		2.1%		-0.1%	

ENERGY AND ELECTRICITY USE IN THE COMMERCIAL SECTOR

	1987		2000		2015	
COLLEGES AND UNIVERSITIES						
floor space, millions sq ft	1,540		1,437		1,656	
avg ann growth, previous 15 years	—		-0.5%		0.9%	
END USE ENERGY INTENSITIES	thousand BTU per square foot annually, percent in form of electricity					
total	93.36	40.4%	90.91	44.6%	80.23	51.8%
space conditioning	49.04	17.8%	45.51	21.1%	38.77	27.7%
ventilation	5.23	100.0%	5.26	100.0%	4.84	100.0%
water heating	9.75	17.9%	9.72	20.3%	7.55	32.0%
cooking	3.80	30.5%	4.31	30.5%	3.27	37.0%
refrigeration	0.58	100.0%	0.66	100.0%	0.60	100.0%
lighting	15.10	100.0%	15.13	100.0%	14.51	100.0%
miscellaneous	9.85	53.1%	10.32	63.8%	10.69	67.9%
END USE ENERGY NEEDS, quadrillion BTU						
total requirements	0.14		0.13		0.13	
fossil/renewables	0.09		0.07		0.07	
electricity	0.06		0.06		0.07	
avg ann growth, previous 15 years						
total end use energy	—		-0.7%		0.1%	
electricity (purchased + self gen)	—		0.0%		1.1%	
RETAIL BUILDINGS						
floor space, millions sq ft	12,190		16,148		18,828	
avg ann growth, previous 15 years	—		2.2%		1.0%	
END USE ENERGY INTENSITIES	thousand BTU per square foot annually, percent in form of electricity					
total	86.58	46.1%	80.31	52.7%	77.67	51.7%
space conditioning	54.16	22.2%	47.24	27.4%	45.68	24.7%
ventilation	4.11	100.0%	4.15	100.0%	3.99	100.0%
water heating	4.99	17.7%	4.40	23.9%	3.93	27.4%
cooking	0.56	26.0%	0.51	34.5%	0.46	46.8%
refrigeration	1.25	100.0%	1.29	100.0%	1.24	100.0%
lighting	16.95	100.0%	17.06	100.0%	16.44	100.0%
miscellaneous	4.55	100.0%	5.67	100.0%	5.93	100.0%
END USE ENERGY NEEDS, quadrillion BTU						
total requirements	1.06		1.30		1.47	
fossil/renewables	0.57		0.64		0.76	
electricity	0.49		0.68		0.76	
avg ann growth, previous 15 years						
total end use energy	—		1.6%		0.8%	
electricity (purchased + self gen)	—		2.6%		0.7%	

ENERGY AND ELECTRICITY USE IN THE COMMERCIAL SECTOR

	1987		2000		2015	
WAREHOUSES						
floor space, millions sq ft	7,620		9,502		10,552	
avg ann growth, previous 15 years	—		1.7%		0.7%	
END USE ENERGY INTENSITIES	thousand BTU per square foot annually, percent in form of electricity					
total	78.05	37.8%	70.92	45.9%	67.91	47.0%
space conditioning	44.93	11.5%	36.45	17.5%	34.89	17.2%
ventilation	3.40	100.0%	3.48	100.0%	3.33	100.0%
water heating	4.30	19.1%	4.22	21.2%	3.64	26.1%
cooking	0.00	0.0%	0.00	0.0%	0.00	0.0%
refrigeration	6.93	100.0%	7.86	100.0%	7.99	100.0%
lighting	9.63	100.0%	9.75	100.0%	9.42	100.0%
miscellaneous	8.86	39.7%	9.16	45.6%	8.62	48.6%
END USE ENERGY NEEDS, quadrillion BTU						
total requirements	0.59		0.67		0.72	
fossil/renewables	0.37		0.36		0.38	
electricity	0.22		0.31		0.34	
avg ann growth, previous 15 years						
total end use energy	—		1.0%		0.4%	
electricity (purchased + self gen)	—		2.5%		0.6%	
MISCELLANEOUS BUILDINGS						
floor space, millions sq ft	13,010		16,267		19,080	
avg ann growth, previous 15 years	—		1.7%		1.1%	
END USE ENERGY INTENSITIES	thousand BTU per square foot annually, percent in form of electricity					
total	82.56	37.7%	76.26	44.7%	72.38	45.2%
space conditioning	54.91	20.9%	47.93	27.4%	45.13	26.6%
ventilation	3.99	100.0%	4.07	100.0%	3.87	100.0%
water heating	2.87	24.0%	2.74	29.7%	2.54	33.4%
cooking	0.89	38.6%	0.81	43.0%	0.79	46.8%
refrigeration	0.83	100.0%	0.87	100.0%	0.80	100.0%
lighting	9.21	100.0%	9.24	100.0%	8.91	100.0%
miscellaneous	9.86	46.1%	10.60	53.2%	10.34	57.4%
END USE ENERGY NEEDS, quadrillion BTU						
total requirements	1.07		1.24		1.38	
fossil/renewables	0.67		0.69		0.76	
electricity	0.40		0.55		0.62	
avg ann growth, previous 15 years						
total end use energy	—		1.1%		0.7%	
electricity (purchased + self gen)	—		2.5%		0.8%	

ENERGY AND ELECTRICITY USE IN THE INDUSTRIAL SECTOR

	1987		2000		2015	
INDUSTRY TOTAL						
value of output, billions 1977$	2,018.3		2,974.6		4,215.8	
avg ann growth, previous 15 years	—			3.0%		2.4%
END USE ENERGY INTENSITIES *thousand BTU per 1977$ of output, percent in form of electricity*						
total	8.58	18.6%	7.60	20.9%	6.81	23.3%
motor drive	1.06	100.0%	1.02	100.0%	0.99	100.0%
electrolysis	0.19	100.0%	0.19	100.0%	0.17	100.0%
lighting & other devices	0.15	100.0%	0.14	100.0%	0.14	100.0%
process heat	7.18	2.8%	6.24	3.7%	5.50	5.0%
END USE ENERGY NEEDS *quadrillion BTU*						
total requirements	17.438		22.727		28.878	
fossil/renewables	14.492		18.416		22.909	
electricity	3.225		4.723		6.679	
avg ann growth, previous 15 years						
total end use energy	—			2.1%		1.6%
electricity (purchased + self gen)	—			3.0%		2.3%
MANUFACTURING TOTAL						
(SIC 20-39)						
value of output, billions 1977$	1,647.6		2,516.3		3,608.1	
avg ann growth, previous 15 years	—			3.3%		2.4%
END USE ENERGY INTENSITIES *thousand BTU per 1977$ of output, percent in form of electricity*						
total	8.45	18.6%	7.47	21.0%	6.70	23.4%
motor drive	1.07	100.0%	1.03	100.0%	1.01	100.0%
electrolysis	0.24	100.0%	0.22	100.0%	0.20	100.0%
lighting & other devices	0.14	100.0%	0.14	100.0%	0.14	100.0%
process heat	7.01	1.8%	6.07	2.9%	5.36	4.2%
END USE ENERGY NEEDS *quadrillion BTU*						
total requirements	14.025		18.903		24.355	
fossil/renewables	11.685		15.330		19.353	
electricity	2.588		3.950		5.665	
avg ann growth, previous 15 years						
total end use energy	—			2.3%		1.7%
electricity (purchased + self gen)	—			3.3%		2.4%

ENERGY AND ELECTRICITY USE IN THE INDUSTRIAL SECTOR

	1987		2000		2015	
AGRICULTURE						
value of output, billions 1977$	150.0		177.9		238.1	
avg ann growth, previous 15 years	—			1.3%		2.0%
END USE ENERGY INTENSITIES thousand BTU per 1977$ of output, percent in form of electricity						
total	5.67	18.2%	5.23	20.4%	4.76	23.3%
END USE ENERGY NEEDS quadrillion BTU						
total requirements	0.851		0.930		1.134	
fossil/renewables	0.696		0.740		0.870	
electricity	0.155		0.190		0.264	
avg ann growth, previous 15 years						
total end use energy	—			0.7%		1.3%
electricity (purchased + self gen)	—			1.6%		2.2%
MINING						
value of output, billions 1977$	85.5		101.7		127.9	
avg ann growth, previous 15 years	—			1.3%		1.5%
END USE ENERGY INTENSITIES thousand BTU per 1977$ of output, percent in form of electricity						
total	21.72	24.2%	20.09	26.5%	18.38	29.4%
END USE ENERGY NEEDS quadrillion BTU						
total requirements	1.870		2.055		2.362	
fossil/renewables	1.451		1.550		1.716	
electricity	0.449		0.541		0.692	
avg ann growth, previous 15 years						
total end use energy	—			0.7%		0.9%
electricity (purchased + self gen)	—			1.4%		1.7%
CONSTRUCTION						
value of output, billions 1977$	135.2		178.7		241.7	
avg ann growth, previous 15 years	—			2.2%		2.0%
END USE ENERGY INTENSITIES thousand BTU per 1977$ of output, percent in form of electricity						
total	5.12	4.7%	4.70	5.2%	4.25	5.7%
END USE ENERGY NEEDS quadrillion BTU						
total requirements	0.693		0.839		1.027	
fossil/renewables	0.660		0.796		0.969	
electricity	0.033		0.043		0.058	
avg ann growth, previous 15 years						
total end use energy	—			1.5%		1.4%
electricity (purchased + self gen)	—			2.1%		2.0%

ENERGY AND ELECTRICITY USE IN THE INDUSTRIAL SECTOR

	1987		2000		2015	
FOOD & KINDRED PRODUCTS						
SIC 20						
value of output, billions 1977$	229.1		277.3		362.7	
avg ann growth, previous 15 years	—		1.5%		1.8%	
END USE ENERGY INTENSITIES thousand BTU per 1977$ of output, percent in form of electricity						
total	3.92	18.6%	3.63	19.8%	3.33	21.4%
motor drive	0.64	100.0%	0.63	100.0%	0.62	100.0%
electrolysis	0.00	100.0%	0.00	100.0%	0.00	100.0%
lighting & other devices	0.08	100.0%	0.08	100.0%	0.08	100.0%
process heat	3.19	0.1%	2.91	0.1%	2.62	0.3%
END USE ENERGY NEEDS quadrillion BTU						
total requirements	0.902		1.011		1.213	
fossil/renewables	0.745		0.825		0.981	
electricity	0.167		0.199		0.258	
avg ann growth, previous 15 years						
total end use energy	—		0.9%		1.2%	
electricity (purchased + self gen)	—		1.4%		1.7%	
TOBACCO PRODUCTS						
SIC 21						
value of output, billions 1977$	14.8		19.3		25.2	
avg ann growth, previous 15 years	—		2.0%		1.8%	
END USE ENERGY INTENSITIES thousand BTU per 1977$ of output, percent in form of electricity						
total	1.63	23.5%	1.52	25.0%	1.40	26.8%
motor drive	0.23	100.0%	0.23	100.0%	0.22	100.0%
electrolysis	0.00	100.0%	0.00	100.0%	0.00	100.0%
lighting & other devices	0.15	100.0%	0.15	100.0%	0.15	100.0%
process heat	1.25	0.0%	1.14	0.0%	1.03	0.0%
END USE ENERGY NEEDS quadrillion BTU						
total requirements	0.024		0.029		0.035	
fossil/renewables	0.019		0.022		0.026	
electricity	0.006		0.007		0.009	
avg ann growth, previous 15 years						
total end use energy	—		1.5%		1.3%	
electricity (purchased + self gen)	—		2.0%		1.7%	

ENERGY AND ELECTRICITY USE IN THE INDUSTRIAL SECTOR

	1987		2000		2015	
TEXTILE MILL PRODUCTS						
SIC 22						
value of output, billions 1977$	49.7		68.2		92.6	
avg ann growth, previous 15 years	—			2.5%		2.1%
END USE ENERGY INTENSITIES thousand BTU per 1977$ of output, percent in form of electricity						
total	5.27	35.4%	4.95	37.5%	4.60	40.3%
motor drive	1.57	100.0%	1.54	100.0%	1.51	100.0%
electrolysis	0.00	100.0%	0.00	100.0%	0.00	100.0%
lighting & other devices	0.28	100.0%	0.28	100.0%	0.28	100.0%
process heat	3.42	0.5%	3.12	1.0%	2.81	2.2%
END USE ENERGY NEEDS quadrillion BTU						
total requirements	0.262		0.338		0.427	
fossil/renewables	0.171		0.213		0.257	
electricity	0.092		0.127		0.171	
avg ann growth, previous 15 years						
total end use energy	—			2.0%		1.6%
electricity (purchased + self gen)	—			2.4%		2.1%
APPAREL & TEXTILE PRODUCTS						
SIC 23						
value of output, billions 1977$	44.5		57.4		76.4	
avg ann growth, previous 15 years	—			2.0%		1.9%
END USE ENERGY INTENSITIES thousand BTU per 1977$ of output, percent in form of electricity						
total	1.12	43.2%	1.05	45.6%	0.99	48.5%
motor drive	0.36	100.0%	0.35	100.0%	0.34	100.0%
electrolysis	0.00	100.0%	0.00	100.0%	0.00	100.0%
lighting & other devices	0.12	100.0%	0.12	100.0%	0.12	100.0%
process heat	0.64	1.1%	0.58	2.0%	0.53	3.4%
END USE ENERGY NEEDS quadrillion BTU						
total requirements	0.050		0.060		0.076	
fossil/renewables	0.028		0.033		0.039	
electricity	0.021		0.028		0.037	
avg ann growth, previous 15 years						
total end use energy	—			1.5%		1.5%
electricity (purchased + self gen)	—			2.0%		1.9%

ENERGY AND ELECTRICITY USE IN THE INDUSTRIAL SECTOR

	1987		2000		2015	
LUMBER & WOOD PRODUCTS **SIC 24**						
value of output, billions 1977$	52.2		73.4		103.7	
avg ann growth, previous 15 years	—			2.7%		2.3%
END USE ENERGY INTENSITIES *thousand BTU per 1977$ of output, percent in form of electricity*						
total	4.22	29.2%	3.93	32.1%	3.63	36.0%
motor drive	1.05	100.0%	1.03	100.0%	1.01	100.0%
electrolysis	0.00	100.0%	0.00	100.0%	0.00	100.0%
lighting & other devices	0.10	100.0%	0.10	100.0%	0.10	100.0%
process heat	3.07	2.5%	2.80	4.6%	2.52	7.7%
END USE ENERGY NEEDS *quadrillion BTU*						
total requirements	0.221		0.289		0.378	
fossil/renewables	0.158		0.199		0.247	
electricity	0.064		0.093		0.135	
avg ann growth, previous 15 years						
total end use energy	—			2.1%		1.8%
electricity (purchased + self gen)	—			2.9%		2.6%
FURNITURE & FIXTURES **SIC 25**						
value of output, billions 1977$	21.2		29.8		43.4	
avg ann growth, previous 15 years	—			2.7%		2.5%
END USE ENERGY INTENSITIES *thousand BTU per 1977$ of output, percent in form of electricity*						
total	2.43	31.7%	2.27	33.4%	2.11	35.4%
motor drive	0.59	100.0%	0.58	100.0%	0.57	100.0%
electrolysis	0.00	100.0%	0.00	100.0%	0.00	100.0%
lighting & other devices	0.18	100.0%	0.18	100.0%	0.18	100.0%
process heat	1.66	0.0%	1.51	0.0%	1.36	0.0%
END USE ENERGY NEEDS *quadrillion BTU*						
total requirements	0.051		0.068		0.092	
fossil/renewables	0.035		0.045		0.059	
electricity	0.016		0.023		0.032	
avg ann growth, previous 15 years						
total end use energy	—			2.1%		2.0%
electricity (purchased + self gen)	—			2.6%		2.4%

ENERGY AND ELECTRICITY USE IN THE INDUSTRIAL SECTOR

	1987		2000		2015	
PAPER & ALLIED PRODUCTS						
SIC 26						
value of output, billions 1977$	69.4		96.4		135.2	
avg ann growth, previous 15 years	—			2.6%		2.3%
END USE ENERGY INTENSITIES thousand BTU per 1977$ of output, percent in form of electricity						
total	35.28	12.7%	32.52	13.5%	29.63	14.6%
motor drive	4.08	100.0%	4.01	100.0%	3.93	100.0%
electrolysis	0.00	100.0%	0.00	100.0%	0.00	100.0%
lighting & other devices	0.39	100.0%	0.39	100.0%	0.39	100.0%
process heat	30.81	0.0%	28.13	0.0%	25.31	0.0%
END USE ENERGY NEEDS quadrillion BTU						
total requirements	2.497		3.188		4.070	
fossil/renewables	2.305		2.932		3.741	
electricity	0.310		0.423		0.584	
avg ann growth, previous 15 years						
total end use energy	—			1.9%		1.6%
electricity (purchased + self gen)	—			2.4%		2.2%
PRINTING & PUBLISHING						
SIC 27						
value of output, billions 1977$	71.7		98.2		137.0	
avg ann growth, previous 15 years	—			2.4%		2.2%
END USE ENERGY INTENSITIES thousand BTU per 1977$ of output, percent in form of electricity						
total	1.43	44.7%	1.35	46.9%	1.27	49.6%
motor drive	0.46	100.0%	0.46	100.0%	0.45	100.0%
electrolysis	0.00	100.0%	0.00	100.0%	0.00	100.0%
lighting & other devices	0.17	100.0%	0.17	100.0%	0.17	100.0%
process heat	0.79	0.7%	0.72	1.2%	0.65	2.0%
END USE ENERGY NEEDS quadrillion BTU						
total requirements	0.102		0.133		0.174	
fossil/renewables	0.057		0.070		0.088	
electricity	0.046		0.062		0.086	
avg ann growth, previous 15 years						
total end use energy	—			2.0%		1.8%
electricity (purchased + self gen)	—			2.4%		2.2%

ENERGY AND ELECTRICITY USE IN THE INDUSTRIAL SECTOR

	1987		2000		2015	
CHEMICALS & ALLIED PRODUCTS **SIC 28**						
value of output, billions 1977$	154.8		238.8		336.9	
avg ann growth, previous 15 years	—			3.4%		2.3%
END USE ENERGY INTENSITIES thousand BTU per 1977$ of output, percent in form of electricity						
total	17.07	19.6%	15.82	20.9%	14.51	22.4%
motor drive	2.17	100.0%	2.13	100.0%	2.09	100.0%
electrolysis	0.87	100.0%	0.85	100.0%	0.84	100.0%
lighting & other devices	0.32	100.0%	0.32	100.0%	0.32	100.0%
process heat	13.72	0.0%	12.53	0.0%	11.27	0.1%
END USE ENERGY NEEDS quadrillion BTU						
total requirements	2.670		3.814		4.945	
fossil/renewables	2.216		3.136		4.074	
electricity	0.519		0.789		1.094	
avg ann growth, previous 15 years						
total end use energy	—			2.8%		1.7%
electricity (purchased + self gen)	—			3.3%		2.2%
PETROLEUM & COAL PRODUCTS **SIC 29**						
value of output, billions 1977$	100.6		132.3		179.7	
avg ann growth, previous 15 years	—			2.1%		2.1%
END USE ENERGY INTENSITIES thousand BTU per 1977$ of output, percent in form of electricity						
total	24.26	6.0%	22.24	6.4%	20.14	7.0%
motor drive	1.35	100.0%	1.33	100.0%	1.30	100.0%
electrolysis	0.00	100.0%	0.00	100.0%	0.00	100.0%
lighting & other devices	0.10	100.0%	0.10	100.0%	0.10	100.0%
process heat	22.80	0.0%	20.81	0.0%	18.73	0.0%
END USE ENERGY NEEDS quadrillion BTU						
total requirements	2.450		2.954		3.633	
fossil/renewables	2.329		2.799		3.440	
electricity	0.147		0.189		0.253	
avg ann growth, previous 15 years						
total end use energy	—			1.4%		1.4%
electricity (purchased + self gen)	—			2.0%		1.9%

ENERGY AND ELECTRICITY USE IN THE INDUSTRIAL SECTOR

	1987		2000		2015	
RUBBER & MISC PLASTICS						
SIC 30						
value of output, billions 1977$	64.2		112.0		170.0	
avg ann growth, previous 15 years	—			4.4%		2.8%
END USE ENERGY INTENSITIES thousand BTU per 1977$ of output, percent in form of electricity						
total	4.37	41.6%	4.11	44.1%	3.84	46.8%
motor drive	1.57	100.0%	1.54	100.0%	1.51	100.0%
electrolysis	0.00	100.0%	0.00	100.0%	0.00	100.0%
lighting & other devices	0.15	100.0%	0.15	100.0%	0.15	100.0%
process heat	2.65	3.8%	2.42	5.2%	2.18	6.3%
END USE ENERGY NEEDS quadrillion BTU						
total requirements	0.281		0.461		0.653	
fossil/renewables	0.164		0.258		0.348	
electricity	0.116		0.204		0.306	
avg ann growth, previous 15 years						
total end use energy	—			3.9%		2.4%
electricity (purchased + self gen)	—			4.4%		2.8%
LEATHER & LEATHER PRODUCTS						
SIC 31						
value of output, billions 1977$	5.7		6.9		7.7	
avg ann growth, previous 15 years	—			1.6%		0.7%
END USE ENERGY INTENSITIES thousand BTU per 1977$ of output, percent in form of electricity						
total	2.24	26.2%	2.09	27.8%	1.93	29.7%
motor drive	0.34	100.0%	0.34	100.0%	0.33	100.0%
electrolysis	0.00	100.0%	0.00	100.0%	0.00	100.0%
lighting & other devices	0.24	100.0%	0.24	100.0%	0.24	100.0%
process heat	1.66	0.0%	1.51	0.0%	1.36	0.0%
END USE ENERGY NEEDS quadrillion BTU						
total requirements	0.013		0.014		0.015	
fossil/renewables	0.009		0.010		0.010	
electricity	0.003		0.004		0.004	
avg ann growth, previous 15 years						
total end use energy	—			1.0%		0.2%
electricity (purchased + self gen)	—			1.5%		0.6%

ENERGY AND ELECTRICITY USE IN THE INDUSTRIAL SECTOR

	1987		2000		2015	
STONE, CLAY, & GLASS **SIC 32**						
value of output, billions 1977$	37.4		56.3		79.0	
avg ann growth, previous 15 years	—			3.2%		2.3%
END USE ENERGY INTENSITIES thousand BTU per 1977$ of output, percent in form of electricity						
total	25.59	12.6%	23.56	14.3%	21.44	16.7%
motor drive	2.72	100.0%	2.68	100.0%	2.62	100.0%
electrolysis	0.00	100.0%	0.00	100.0%	0.00	100.0%
lighting & other devices	0.17	100.0%	0.17	100.0%	0.17	100.0%
process heat	22.69	1.4%	20.71	2.5%	18.64	4.2%
END USE ENERGY NEEDS quadrillion BTU						
total requirements	0.957		1.328		1.694	
fossil/renewables	0.838		1.140		1.415	
electricity	0.120		0.190		0.283	
avg ann growth, previous 15 years						
total end use energy	—			2.6%		1.6%
electricity (purchased + self gen)	—			3.6%		2.7%
PRIMARY METALS INDUSTRIES **SIC 33**						
value of output, billions 1977$	86.9		130.1		184.2	
avg ann growth, previous 15 years	—			3.1%		2.3%
END USE ENERGY INTENSITIES thousand BTU per 1977$ of output, percent in form of electricity						
total	25.21	20.8%	23.20	23.4%	20.93	27.2%
motor drive	1.28	100.0%	1.26	100.0%	1.24	100.0%
electrolysis	2.83	100.0%	2.65	100.0%	2.31	100.0%
lighting & other devices	0.26	100.0%	0.26	100.0%	0.26	100.0%
process heat	20.84	4.2%	19.02	6.6%	17.12	11.0%
END USE ENERGY NEEDS quadrillion BTU						
total requirements	2.202		3.030		3.876	
fossil/renewables	1.770		2.364		2.913	
electricity	0.456		0.706		1.047	
avg ann growth, previous 15 years						
total end use energy	—			2.5%		1.7%
electricity (purchased + self gen)	—			3.4%		2.7%

ENERGY AND ELECTRICITY USE IN THE INDUSTRIAL SECTOR

	1987		2000		2015	
FABRICATED METAL PRODUCTS						
SIC 34						
value of output, billions 1977$	100.2		150.1		211.1	
avg ann growth, previous 15 years	—			3.2%		2.3%
END USE ENERGY INTENSITIES *thousand BTU per 1977$ of output, percent in form of electricity*						
total	3.33	30.7%	3.15	36.4%	2.95	40.7%
motor drive	0.45	100.0%	0.44	100.0%	0.43	100.0%
electrolysis	0.00	100.0%	0.00	100.0%	0.00	100.0%
lighting & other devices	0.07	100.0%	0.07	100.0%	0.07	100.0%
process heat	2.81	18.2%	2.64	24.3%	2.46	28.7%
END USE ENERGY NEEDS *quadrillion BTU*						
total requirements	0.333		0.473		0.624	
ossil/renewables	0.231		0.301		0.371	
electricity	0.102		0.172		0.253	
avg ann growth, previous 15 years						
total end use energy	—			2.7%		1.9%
electricity (purchased + self gen)	—			4.1%		2.6%
NON-ELECTRICAL MACHINERY						
SIC 35						
value of output, billions 1977$	144.7		289.1		442.9	
avg ann growth, previous 15 years	—			5.5%		2.9%
END USE ENERGY INTENSITIES *thousand BTU per 1977$ of output, percent in form of electricity*						
total	1.91	38.0%	1.82	41.5%	1.72	44.3%
motor drive	0.50	100.0%	0.49	100.0%	0.48	100.0%
electrolysis	0.00	100.0%	0.00	100.0%	0.00	100.0%
lighting & other devices	0.08	100.0%	0.08	100.0%	0.08	100.0%
process heat	1.33	11.1%	1.25	14.8%	1.16	17.5%
END USE ENERGY NEEDS *quadrillion BTU*						
total requirements	0.277		0.526		0.763	
fossil/renewables	0.172		0.309		0.426	
electricity	0.105		0.218		0.338	
avg ann growth, previous 15 years						
total end use energy	—			5.1%		2.5%
electricity (purchased + self gen)	—			5.8%		3.0%

ENERGY AND ELECTRICITY USE IN THE INDUSTRIAL SECTOR

	1987		2000		2015	
ELECTRICAL EQUIPMENT						
SIC 36						
value of output, billions 1977$	141.7		280.2		442.9	
avg ann growth, previous 15 years		—		5.4%		3.1%
END USE ENERGY INTENSITIES *thousand BTU per 1977$ of output, percent in form of electricity*						
total	1.72	49.5%	1.65	50.9%	1.58	52.4%
motor drive	0.73	100.0%	0.72	100.0%	0.70	100.0%
electrolysis	0.00	100.0%	0.00	100.0%	0.00	100.0%
lighting & other devices	0.11	100.0%	0.11	100.0%	0.11	100.0%
process heat	0.88	1.3%	0.83	1.7%	0.77	2.1%
END USE ENERGY NEEDS *quadrillion BTU*						
total requirements	0.244		0.463		0.700	
fossil/renewables	0.123		0.228		0.334	
electricity	0.120		0.236		0.367	
avg ann growth, previous 15 years						
total end use energy		—		5.1%		2.8%
electricity (purchased + self gen)		—		5.3%		3.0%
TRANSPORTATION EQUIPMENT						
SIC 37						
value of output, billions 1977$	200.6		301.8		428.5	
avg ann growth, previous 15 years		—		3.2%		2.4%
END USE ENERGY INTENSITIES *thousand BTU per 1977$ of output, percent in form of electricity*						
total	1.85	36.5%	1.76	40.3%	1.66	43.3%
motor drive	0.43	100.0%	0.42	100.0%	0.42	100.0%
electrolysis	0.04	100.0%	0.04	100.0%	0.04	100.0%
lighting & other devices	0.04	100.0%	0.04	100.0%	0.04	100.0%
process heat	1.34	12.4%	1.26	16.6%	1.17	19.6%
END USE ENERGY NEEDS *quadrillion BTU*						
total requirements	0.372		0.532		0.713	
fossil/renewables	0.236		0.318		0.405	
electricity	0.135		0.214		0.309	
avg ann growth, previous 15 years						
total end use energy		—		2.8%		2.0%
electricity (purchased + self gen)		—		3.6%		2.5%

ENERGY AND ELECTRICITY USE IN THE INDUSTRIAL SECTOR

	1987		2000		2015	

INSTRUMENTS & RELATED PRODUCTS
SIC 38

	1987		2000		2015	
value of output, billions 1977$	39.0		69.0		107.0	
avg ann growth, previous 15 years	—			4.5%		3.0%

END USE ENERGY INTENSITIES   thousand BTU per 1977$ of output, percent in form of electricity

total	2.18	32.0%	2.07	33.0%	1.96	34.2%
motor drive	0.65	100.0%	0.64	100.0%	0.62	100.0%
electrolysis	0.00	100.0%	0.00	100.0%	0.00	100.0%
lighting & other devices	0.05	100.0%	0.05	100.0%	0.05	100.0%
process heat	1.48	0.0%	1.39	0.0%	1.29	0.0%

END USE ENERGY NEEDS   quadrillion BTU

total requirements	0.085		0.143		0.210	
fossil/renewables	0.058		0.096		0.138	
electricity	0.027		0.047		0.072	

avg ann growth, previous 15 years						
total end use energy	—			4.1%		2.6%
electricity (purchased + self gen)	—			4.4%		2.8%

MISC MANUFACTURING
SIC 39

	1987		2000		2015	
value of output, billions 1977$	19.2		29.8		42.0	
avg ann growth, previous 15 years	—			3.4%		2.3%

END USE ENERGY INTENSITIES   thousand BTU per 1977$ of output, percent in form of electricity

total	1.72	36.8%	1.64	37.9%	1.56	39.2%
motor drive	0.57	100.0%	0.56	100.0%	0.55	100.0%
electrolysis	0.00	100.0%	0.00	100.0%	0.00	100.0%
lighting & other devices	0.06	100.0%	0.06	100.0%	0.06	100.0%
process heat	1.09	0.0%	1.02	0.0%	0.95	0.0%

END USE ENERGY NEEDS   quadrillion BTU

total requirements	0.033		0.049		0.065	
fossil/renewables	0.021		0.030		0.040	
electricity	0.012		0.018		0.025	

avg ann growth, previous 15 years						
total end use energy	—			3.1%		2.0%
electricity (purchased + self gen)	—			3.3%		2.2%

TRANSPORTATION SECTOR FORECAST RESULTS

THE REFERENCE CASE SCENARIO

all figures in quadrillilion Btu

Year	Total	Fossil	Electricity total	rail	pipeline	vehicles*
HISTORY						
1980	19.74	19.659	0.081	0.013	0.068	0.000
1981	19.54	19.458	0.082	0.013	0.069	0.000
1982	19.11	19.029	0.080	0.013	0.067	0.000
1983	19.18	19.097	0.083	0.013	0.070	0.000
1984	19.92	19.840	0.085	0.015	0.070	0.000
1985	20.16	20.077	0.088	0.015	0.072	0.000
1986	20.82	20.734	0.090	0.016	0.074	0.000
1987	21.32	21.229	0.090	0.016	0.074	0.000
REFERENCE CASE FORECAST						
1988	21.52	21.430	0.093	0.016	0.076	0.000
1989	21.73	21.633	0.095	0.017	0.078	0.000
1990	21.94	21.839	0.098	0.017	0.080	0.000
1991	22.15	22.046	0.100	0.018	0.082	0.000
1992	22.36	22.255	0.103	0.018	0.085	0.000
1993	22.55	22.445	0.105	0.019	0.087	0.000
1994	22.74	22.636	0.108	0.019	0.089	0.000
1995	22.94	22.830	0.111	0.019	0.091	0.000
1996	23.14	23.025	0.114	0.020	0.093	0.000
1997	23.34	23.221	0.117	0.020	0.096	0.001
1998	23.54	23.420	0.120	0.021	0.098	0.001
1999	23.74	23.620	0.123	0.022	0.100	0.001
2000	24.09	23.964	0.126	0.022	0.103	0.001
2001	24.36	24.232	0.129	0.023	0.105	0.002
2002	24.63	24.502	0.133	0.023	0.107	0.002
2003	24.91	24.776	0.136	0.023	0.110	0.003
2004	25.19	25.052	0.140	0.024	0.112	0.004
2005	25.48	25.332	0.144	0.024	0.114	0.005
2006	25.76	25.615	0.148	0.025	0.117	0.006
2007	26.05	25.901	0.152	0.026	0.119	0.007
2008	26.35	26.190	0.156	0.026	0.122	0.008
2009	26.64	26.482	0.161	0.027	0.124	0.010
2010	26.94	26.778	0.166	0.027	0.127	0.011
2011	27.25	27.076	0.170	0.028	0.130	0.013
2012	27.55	27.379	0.176	0.028	0.133	0.015
2013	27.87	27.684	0.181	0.029	0.135	0.016
2014	28.18	27.993	0.186	0.030	0.138	0.018
2015	28.50	28.306	0.191	0.030	0.141	0.020

* Includes contributions from the following:
Sub-compact auto for private transportation, 100 mile range per charge.
• Fleet van for commercial sector, 60 mile range per charge.
• Fleet van for commercial sector, 120 mile range per charge.
• Equivalent of conventional automobile for private transportation.